Praise for **SN**

"Bill Johnson has endured more in his lifetime than most could imagine. And yet, what amazed me most in reading *Snow Blind* was not that he survived being shot in the head or that he relearned to live a remarkably normal life afterward, but the fact that he simply refused to allow someone else's actions to steal the possibility of his future. In a society where excuses are offered for poor behavior or lousy results, Bill casts a wildly different vision of taking total ownership for our lives and embracing the limitless possibilities within them. Read this book."

—JOHN O'LEARY

#1 National Bestselling author of *In Awe* and *On Fire*

———

"A victim of a random shooting on a business trip, Bill Johnson was blinded while his two business companions suffered mortal wounds. Although he realized he had challenges to face, Bill showed bold determination to return to the life he led as a businessman, a father, and a lover of life. He miraculously skipped typical phases of grief to regain his status and venture out to new experiences. Bill's inspirational journey shows that a powerful drive can surmount all odds and that someone who becomes blinded can live a fulfilling life. I consider Bill a role model not only for blind people but for all those who are fighting not to allow overwhelming challenges to interfere with the dreams for their lives."

—CARL AUGUSTO

President Emeritus of the American Foundation for the Blind

"Bill takes us on a journey from the moment of near devastation to a life of learning to adapt. His steadfast determination allowed him to constantly push the envelope and attain his goals. I recommend this book to anyone looking for the steps to take in order to get their life back on track."

—WALT SUTTON
Senior Manager of Instruction and Training for The Seeing Eye

---

"An unbelievable story about an incredible man. This story is truly the triumph of good over evil. Heartbreaking, addicting, and heartwarming all in one book."

—MICHAEL SUMMERS, MS
Exercise Physiologist, Sports Performance Coach

"Bill Johnson's narrative puts us into the world of a man blinded after living forty-one years as a sighted person. In his description of the events that led to his blindness, he takes the reader inside the experience, giving a minute-by-minute feel of the disorientation and confusion of the violent assault that took his sight and the lives of two of his colleagues. His account of his rehabilitation and learning to live his life in an entirely different manner is inspiring reading for anyone who hopes to understand those who navigate the world without sight. Bill's determination and independence are models to be admired and mimicked by any of us who find ourselves confronted by an abrupt life change."

—JACK BARNETT
Retired Counselor and Friend

"Bill Johnson is one of the most courageous people I've ever met. I'm struck by the aggressive fashion in which he chooses to face adversity and grow. He inspires all who know him."

—TIB ALBACH
Saint Louis, Missouri

———▬———

"Bill has taught us that hurdles are part of life and that acceptance is the key. He exudes a contagious, positive attitude and outlook on life that is filled with gratitude and a ton of humor. This book is a touching story of how a man who lost his sight has lived his life as if he has zero handicaps."

—TOM ERICKSON
Retired KPMG Partner

———▬———

"I could not stop reading! Bill's storytelling takes you right along on the journey with him, and I was captivated from the first few words. Bill's independence and determination shone through immediately. He refused to let his sudden blindness hold him back from living the life he always intended to live. Bill is an inspiration to anyone who has fought through hard times and he is one heck of a snow skier. Keep it up!"

—CHRISTINE HOLMBERG
Executive Director, Foresight Ski Guides

"An incredibly uplifting read and great example to all of us about the power of perseverance and having a positive attitude when staring down great adversity."

—DOUG WHITE
Former Partner, KPMG/Managing Director, BearingPoint

———▬———

"Reading this book brought back a flood of memories during that horrific time in Atlanta. It was a surreal experience for me as an outsider, who got to peek into this family's dynamics and how they dealt with this unspeakable tragedy. What was inspiring for me during that time—and after reading this book—was how Bill Johnson dealt with his new life in a gracious and disciplined way, while making others feel comfortable with his new-found disability. He continues to be an inspiration to all of us. By the way, I married Bill's sister a few months after the event!"

—RICH DAMARO
Brother-in-law, Former KPMG Partner

———▬———

"Bill and I met almost thirteen years ago. I'd heard a lot of his past, but reading this memoir filled in my understanding. Although we didn't know each other at the time, he and I shared the same profession at competing companies for most of the period he describes in the book. This story is, at the same time, wonderful and terrible.

Bill is unbelievably positive, strong, courageous, brave, and resourceful. He also is smart, insightful, introspective, self-aware, and humorous. Bill's descriptions of events paint vivid pictures of his experiences. I felt a range of emotions while reading *Snow Blind*—shock, admiration, sadness, happiness. At times, when reading it, I cried.

Most of the time when I'm around Bill, I feel that I'm with a better person than I am. His memoir only reinforced that. He and his book are inspirational."

—CARL BARNES
Former Price Waterhouse Partner

———————

"I've known Bill for several years. Shortly after we became friends, during a casual discussion, we discovered that we both really enjoy skiing. I was intrigued that someone who was blind could actually ski, and by the end of our discussion, we agreed that we should go on a ski trip. We became ski buddies that took us on several trips to different mountains with some other friends occasionally joining us.

Skiing with Bill is always an inspiration. My favorite thing to do is to ski about thirty or forty yards behind him and watch as his guide and he disappear over a steep black run. I wonder how he does it, even though I've seen it a hundred times! I'm really glad to see Bill tell his story. It's one that definitely needed to be told!"

—MARK STEPHENS
Saint Louis, Missouri

SNOW
BLIND

WILLIAM M. JOHNSON

SNOW BLIND

RECOVERING AFTER THE RANDOM SHOOTING

A MEMOIR

Stonebrook Publishing
Saint Louis, Missouri

A STONEBROOK PUBLISHING BOOK
Copyright ©2021 William M. Johnson

This book was guided in development and
edited by Nancy L. Erickson, The Book Professor®
TheBookProfessor.com

All rights reserved. Published in the United States
by Stonebrook Publishing, a division of Stonebrook Enterprises, LLC,
Saint Louis, Missouri.

Library of Congress Control Number: 2020922827
ISBN: 978-1-7358021-3-8

www.stonebrookpublishing.net

PRINTED IN THE UNITED STATES OF AMERICA

10   9   8   7   6   5   4   3   2   1

*For my late parents, Warren M. Johnson, Jr.
and Doris C. Johnson*

CONTENTS

SNOW BLIND

CHAPTER
ONE

TUESDAY, JULY 2, 1991

WHACK! My head felt like it had been slammed with a baseball bat. I hit the pavement, face down on the Atlanta sidewalk. Everything was black.

I closed my eyes and kept my hands over them. The little bit of light that seeped through caused excruciating pain, like hordes of needles were piercing my eyes. It crossed my mind that I might never be able to see again and that if I lost consciousness, I'd die.

The hard sidewalk pained my knees and elbows. How long had I been here? Oh, *the pain!* Time crawled, and a fleeting thought about Tony and Keith drifted by.

"Chief, how are you doing?" came the loud greeting.

"It hurts," I answered.

"I'm an EMT, and I'm here to help you, Chief. Just lie still and do what I tell you."

He examined me, and I felt myself being lifted onto a stretcher. A younger, less confident male voice said, "I need to cut off your shoes and clothes."

"No way! These are new shoes and a good suit," I joked. But he didn't laugh. He thought I was serious, so I quickly said, "Go ahead and do whatever you need to do." My clothes were soon lying under me and my shoes were gone.

Hands felt all over my body. Chest, abdomen, each arm and leg.

"Does that hurt? How about that?" the EMT asked as his hands flew around.

"My eyes hurt."

"Can you move your arms and legs for me?" I did as he asked.

"Good. Now hold still. This will hurt for a second."

I felt a stab at my wrist, and he said, "I'm giving you some fluid."

He continued to banter with me: "Hang in there Chief;" "Stay with us, Chief;" and finally, "How are you, Chief?"

"OK," I answered. "It hurts."

A new voice chimed in, "What have we got here?"

"Two 45s and a 15," my guy said.

"What does that mean?" I asked.

"Don't worry, Chief. You're the 15. We're taking you first."

The stretcher bumped over the sidewalk and was fed into the ambulance.

"Don't forget my suitcase and briefcase," I called out while I pointed back over my head at who knows what. What did I think—that I was jumping into a cab at the airport?

The siren whooped and the ambulance took off.

"Doing good, Chief. We'll be at the hospital soon," the EMT reassured me.

The drive was quick and the siren wailed the whole way. I kept my eyes shut tight because of the pain. I heard someone in front read my vitals over the radio. His voice was strained, and it struck me that this was an emergency.

"Just a little longer, Chief."

The ambulance screeched to a halt. The doors were flung open, and my stretcher was jerked out. As I was wheeled into the ER, I heard a lot of activity and pressing, urgent voices. Then came the questions.

"Can you lift your left foot? Good. Now try the right. Okay, how about your left hand? Now lift the right one. Do you know what day it is?"

"Tuesday, " I answered

"Who's the President?"

"George Bush."

Someone held my head and said, "Open your eyes for me."

"Oooooh, it hurts." The needles had multiplied.

"Give it a try. Just for a second or two," he said as he examined me.

He gave me a fourteen out of fifteen on the Glascow Coma Scale. My ability to move, feel, and answer questions was fine. But I lost a point because my "pupils were 4mm and nonreactive."

They prepped me for a CAT scan. That was the last thing I remembered.

FRIDAY, JULY 5

I was slowly coming awake. My head felt the crush of a terrible hangover. The beeps and other sounds reminded me of a hospital room on television. *Beep . . . beep . . . beep . . . whoosh.*

I felt all around me and found rails on both sides of the bed. *A hospital bed*, I thought. I rolled slightly toward one side and felt a pull at my wrist—a piece of tape anchored an IV to the back of my right hand. I couldn't see. Everything was pitch black.

Suddenly, a voice pierced the darkness. "Mr. Johnson, are you awake?" she asked.

"Yes."

"Welcome to Grady Memorial Hospital in Atlanta. You'll be just fine," the nurse said. "We're taking good care of you."

What happened to me? I had a distant, hazy recollection of kneeling on the sidewalk, hearing someone say, "Chief, stay with us." *Was there an ambulance?* My thoughts were all jumbled. It seemed so long ago. *How did I get from the ambulance to this place?*

I drifted off again. Many bits of memory.

Another voice interrupted the beeping and whooshing. "Hello Mr. Johnson. I'm Dr. Chris Clare. How do you feel?"

"OK, I guess."

"Can we get anything to make you more comfortable?"

"I don't know. Maybe some water. My mouth is dry."

"Do you have any sharp pain, anywhere?" he asked.

"Not really sharp, but my eyes hurt a lot."

"Do you know what happened to you?"

"A little, but not really," I said.

"Would you like me to tell you?"

"Sure."

"You and your friends were shot by a man on the street." I don't think that was the first time I'd been told this, but it was the first time I'd understood it. *I'd been shot!*

"The bullet hit your head, and your eyesight has been affected. You just rest and we'll take good care of you," he said. "If you need anything, the nurse will be here to help you. Do you have any questions?"

"A bullet hit my head? Where?"

"You were struck in the left temple. The bullet passed behind the orbits of your eyes and exited at your right temple."

"Oh, my God. What have I been doing since then?" I asked.

"You were resting very comfortably until about an hour ago. That's when you pulled out your breathing tube and set off a lot of alarms. You had everyone jumping for a bit."

"Wow. I don't remember that."

"That's normal. You're still pretty medicated. Just relax," he said. "Now that you're awake, we're going to move you to Emory University Hospital."

"What are the medications for?"

"Some for pain, but mostly to reduce the risk of brain swelling and seizures."

I drifted off again.

CHAPTER
TWO

"Hello Mr. Johnson, I'm Rosa, your nurse. Are you awake now?"

"Yeah. Did I ever get that water? My mouth is still dry."

"You just arrived at the Emory Hospital neurosurgical ICU. I'll be happy to get you a drink."

"How are you, pal?" a familiar voice said.

"Dad? Is that you?" I said, reaching out my hand to find his.

"Yes, and Katherine is here too." I was glad that both my father and sister had come.

What day is it?" I asked.

"Friday, July fifth," Katherine answered.

"Huh," I said as I processed that. "Tuesday I was going to the subway." Wow. Three days gone.

"We've been with you since Wednesday. We both flew in when we got the news," Katherine said.

"Where's Mom?"

"She's at home holding down the fort," Dad said. "We've sure been worried about you, Bill. It's great to see you awake and to hear you talking."

"What have you been doing for the past two days?" I asked them.

"Mostly just coming to see you at the other hospital," Katherine said.

"That was pretty boring for a few days, wasn't it?"

"Not really. A nurse told us to talk to you. She said you would know we were there. We held your hand and asked you to squeeze if you could hear what we said, and you finally did."

"Weird. I don't remember that."

"It gave us a little hope that you were still in there."

Soon the doctor came in. "Hello again, Mr. Johnson. I'm Dr. Chris Claire. I saw you at the other hospital, but you were mostly asleep. Are you feeling a little more awake now?"

"I guess so."

"Do you feel up to answering some questions?" he asked.

"Sure."

"First, can you move each of your legs for me?" I did as he asked. "Now each of your arms?"

"Excellent," he said. "Do you know what year this is?"

"1991." His questions made me think of the medical shows I'd seen on TV.

"What month is it?"

"July," I answered.

"Who is President of the United States?"

"George Bush," I said.

"Where do you live?" he asked.

"Saint Louis, Missouri."

"Mr. Johnson, it appears you've suffered no permanent injuries, other than your vision," Dr. Clair said. "You may not think so, but you are actually quite fortunate. Would you like to hear more about what you've gone through?"

"Sure."

"When you arrived at the other hospital, we stabilized you and immediately cleaned out the gunshot wounds at your temples. Those wounds weren't really that difficult to clean. The CT scan showed a very small and minimal subdural hematoma. But when you were in the ICU, it got larger. We caught it immediately, and you were rushed back into the OR late Tuesday night."

"What's a hematoma?" I asked.

"That means there was bleeding in your brain. The blood collects and causes pressure, which is dangerous. When a pool of blood clots, it can cause problems. Your score on the Glascow Coma Scale dropped from fourteen to ten in only twenty minutes, so you were immediately intubated. We increased your oxygen to cut down on brain swelling."

"They told me your vital signs had dropped off the table," Dad interjected.

"We then performed a craniotomy to get to the problems and resolve them."

"Performed a what?" I said.

"A craniotomy. The blood clot was in your brain. We cut out a square of your skull, so we could get to the clot and fix it. Then we put the piece of bone back in place and held it there with staples. If you feel your head, you'll notice some bandages. We've been uncovering the incisions and monitoring their healing for the last several days while you've been sleeping. The healing is going well. There's also a drain line under the bandage, which allows excess fluid to be drained off your brain, so the pressure doesn't build up."

I felt my head. It was a mass of bandages. I also felt a large, boxy contraption over my eyes. "What's this?" I asked as I felt it.

"Those are blackout glasses. In the ER, you said that the light hurt your eyes. The glasses should help."

"How long will I be here?" I asked.

"We have to see how you do and figure out what the next step will be, but you'll probably be in the hospital for a few weeks."

As I fiddled with the blackout glasses, I asked, "What's going on with my eyesight?"

"We're still evaluating that," he said. "You suffered damage to your retinas and optic nerves. There's some swelling of your brain. There's a slight possibility that when the swelling goes down, some vision may return."

Later that afternoon Katherine asked me a question. "Can you tell me what you remember?"

"Tony and I were going to take a cab to the airport, but we were running late," I said. "So Keith suggested that MARTA, the subway, would be faster, and he offered to show us the way."

Tony Lake was my boss, a consulting Partner at KPMG Peat Marwick, and my friend and mentor. Keith Jonas was a Vice President for our client, C&S Sovran Bank. We'd met with him in Atlanta to discuss an ongoing consulting project.

"Keith told us the MARTA station was only a couple of blocks away. When we got close, I thought I heard fireworks over my left shoulder. Pop! Pop! Pop! Pop! I turned my head to look, and it felt like I was hit in the head with a baseball bat. I was knocked to my hands and knees on the sidewalk. I vaguely remember an EMT, an ambulance, and getting to a hospital, but nothing after that. I didn't actually know what had happened until the doctor explained it to me.

Where are Keith and Tony?"

"It's not good," Katherine said. "Are you sure you want to hear this now?"

"I'm sure."

"They were also shot, Bill. Keith died almost immediately. Tony was taken to Grady, like you, but he was too badly injured to survive."

"That's terrible," was all I could say. Tears welled in my eyes. Both these men were extraordinary individuals who'd achieved much in their too-short lives. But, more importantly, they were both genuinely good and honorable men, both with families.

Tony was one of the best people for whom I had ever worked. I had learned so much in the several years we worked together. I already missed him. Even worse, his wife was pregnant and they had a set of five-year-old triplets.

We were all silent for some time, then Dad asked, "Would you like to speak to your mother? I'm sure she would like to talk to you."

"That would be great," I answered.

Katherine got Mom on the line and handed me the receiver.

"Hi Mom," I said.

"How are you doing?" she asked.

"I guess I'm OK. It's nice that Dad and Katherine are here."

"You really had us worried, but you sound good," Mom said. She was always positive.

"You sound good too. I'll talk to you later." I handed the phone back to Katherine.

Within the next day or two, I felt like calling a friend of mine back home. "Could you hand me the phone? I want to make a call." I held out my hand, and Katherine put the handset in it.

"What number do you want to call?" she asked.

"Just hand me the whole phone. I can dial it," I said. I felt the layout of the key pad, pressed nine, and made my call.

"How can you just dial the phone like that?" Katherine asked.

"I used to work for the phone company," I said. "I haven't forgotten how to dial."

It never crossed my mind that I wouldn't be able to dial a phone. Reaching outside the hospital and making that call by myself was rewarding after lying in the hospital bed and having others take care of me. It was the first on a long list of daily living and work-related skills I'd have to re-acquire over the coming months and years. Performing this simple task showed me that I could carry on as an independent person, blind or not. Of course, I also realized that I would occasionally need to ask for help, like asking someone to hand me the phone.

I called my friend, Don, at the Lake of the Ozarks. We owned a cabin together and had planned to spend the Fourth of July holiday with other friends to water ski, fish, and generally enjoy ourselves.

"What's up at the lake, Don?" I greeted him.

"Bill? B. J., is that really you?" he said.

"Yes. How's the weather at the lake?"

"I can't believe I'm talking to you. We're all sitting out on the patio talking about good times at the lake, expecting that we'd never see you again. I can't believe I'm talking to you," he repeated. "The news stories made it sound like you were in really bad shape, but you sound good. Are you OK? Where are you now?"

"I'm in a hospital in Atlanta," I said. "I can't see anything, but otherwise I think I'll be OK."

"From what we heard on the news stories, we didn't think you were going to make it," he said.

"I don't know anything about the news stories, but I'm here."

"I have to go tell everyone else that you called," he said. "This is like getting a call from the grave. But a very good call!" My friends were stunned and elated.

———■———

I fell into the hospital routine, dozing and sleeping a lot. I was hooked up to several devices and tubes, so I could barely roll onto my side. The nurses came and went, asking how I felt and recording my vitals. They also brought me meals—Jell-O and other soft and sweet things. But I wasn't very hungry.

I had not been at Emory very long when a visitor arrived from KPMG Peat Marwick. Apparently the shooting had sent shock waves through the firm, and everyone was eager to support me however they could.

"Hi Bill, I'm Rich from the Atlanta office. If you need anything, or if your family needs anything, just let me know. I'll be around as much as I can. Don't worry about a thing. All you need to think about is getting better and getting out of here."

"Thanks, Rich," I said. "I appreciate that." He seemed like a sincere guy.

Over the next few days, I had a few other visitors and some incoming calls were put through to me. Jon Madonna, the head of KPMG Peat Marwick, and John Gannon, the head of the consulting division both called to offer their condolences and support. Mr. Gannon even suggested that if I couldn't travel and see clients, I could become a guru in my practice area. Not really very realistic, but he meant well. The Mayor of Atlanta, Maynard Jackson, also called to express his sorrow that such violence had happened in his city, and he wished me the best. These calls were a blur to me, as was most of my time in Atlanta.

As I drifted in and out of sleep, it seemed like Dad and Katherine were with me all the time.

"How are you doing, Pal?" Dad would say as he walked past the foot of my bed and squeezed one of my big toes under the sheet. Our family was very loving and supportive, but not very big on hugging, and that gesture meant a lot to me. I sensed from our conversations that he was shaken by the week's events and that he would rather give up his own life than for me to go through this and face the future he pictured. The squeeze was his "hug" for me, and I relished it.

Both Dad and Katherine tried to present an upbeat attitude, but I could tell they were deeply concerned about my prospects—medically and emotionally—immediately and for the rest of my life.

I was still quite drugged, but I knew from the onset that I was still *me*. I didn't focus on the challenges that would confront me when I returned home and built a new life as a blind person. I focused on the fact that I seemed to be all here physically—and more importantly—mentally. I knew I was OK. My mind worked like my mind always had. I had the same thoughts and perspectives about things as always. No crazy thoughts. No memory loss. I was still myself.

One day Dad and Katherine were trying to delicately feel me out about my thoughts regarding my future, specifically rehabilitation and going back to work, among other things.

"I don't think you'll be ready to go home when you get out of the hospital," Katherine said. "So, I've been looking into places you could go for rehabilitation. There are well-known schools in Massachusetts, Illinois, and other places. I've just started my research."

Rehabilitation was, of course, important for me to consider. But I wasn't ready to think about future plans yet.

"Don't worry, " I said. "We'll figure all that out. I remembered seeing blind people ski in Aspen when I was in college. I can't play racquetball anymore, but maybe I'll try snow skiing this winter."

I hadn't gone skiing in ten years, so I'm not sure where that idea came from, but the thought of skiing again stuck with me. That was about the extent of my knowledge of and connection to people who were blind; I'd observed them from a distance on a ski slope.

Katherine was quiet for a moment then said, "That would be nice."

About a week into my stay in Atlanta, I started lobbying to be let out. I thought my injuries were less serious than they were. The treatments mostly involved medications to reduce the risk of seizure, brain swelling, and infection. Oh yeah, and the blindness. They didn't have anything to offer in that department except to hold out the unlikely hope that as my brain swelling decreased, the reduced pressure on the optic nerves might allow some return of vision. I don't know if this theory was actually valid, but fortunately, I didn't cling to that hope.

I wanted to get back home. The house I'd bought three years before had become comfortable for my two kids and me. I was a divorced father of two: my son Chris and my daughter Kelly. When I'd last seen them, they were four and six years old, but while I lay in the hospital in Atlanta, Kelly had celebrated her fifth birthday. I needed to see them both.

I guess I was in denial about my situation, which can be healthy to a point. I think it initially kept me from feeling helplessness or despair. I didn't deny that I couldn't see, but I held an innate belief that my life was on track and would continue to progress forward. I had already experienced life's ups and downs. I always celebrated the successes, and worked my way through the challenges. I couldn't picture my life as a blind person, good or bad, and I didn't have a step-by-step plan for getting from where I was to where I would be. I simply had a core belief that I was OK, and I wanted to take the next step forward. I felt that I needed to get home to gauge my situation and figure out the next step.

My talk of going home prompted a conversation with Dad. "Your mother is cleaning up your old bedroom for you," he said.

"Huh?" I questioned. I had not slept in that bed for twenty years.

"We thought you could move back in with us, so we can help you out. Your mom is looking forward to cooking for more than just the two of us," Dad said.

"I'll think about it," I said.

Mom and Dad still lived in the house I'd grown up in from the age of twelve. It was a very comfortable house, I loved them both, and they were always great parents. But I couldn't see myself being *that guy*. A damaged person who had to move back in with his parents to work back to an independent life—or not. If I moved in with them, how would I ever move out?

I didn't give Dad's suggestion much thought.

I'd always been pretty independent, even a bit of a lone wolf. I'd become adept at letting school, client work, and sometimes my personal life reach the edge of the cliff. And then I'd save the day by doing what needed to be done to put everything right at the last minute. Whether that was the best way to deal with life or not, this self-reliant approach had rarely failed me. This was certainly the biggest cliff I'd ever been on. So, I wanted to get back to my own house and take care of myself, to figure this out on my own. It seemed like the right thing to do, and I didn't waver in my decision.

CHAPTER
THREE

Whether through my lobbying, my family's desire to go home, or (probably) good medical reasons, I was transported to Saint Louis in an air ambulance and admitted to the neurosurgery department at Barnes Hospital—only ten days after the shooting. It felt great to be back in my hometown, even if I was in another hospital. I could picture Barnes Hospital in my mind and could easily envision the drive to my house from there. Those familiar images gave me great comfort.

Dad and Katherine had also flown in the air ambulance. As I got settled, they arrived with my mom.

"Hello, Kiddo," she said.

"Hi, Mom. I'm so glad you're here." I easily recognized her voice.

"You look good," she lied. Much of the swelling had gone down, but my head still held multiple staples, and I was sporting a very bad haircut. Even so, I appreciated her compliment.

After making sure I was in good hands, my family left me in the care of the nurses and doctors. Dad had been away from Mom and his home for ten days. Katherine planned to stay in Saint Louis for the upcoming weekend, but she needed to get back to her life and job in Chicago. Their lives, like mine, had been rudely interrupted and would be altered forever.

Early the first morning, I heard a knock at my door.

"Hello, who is it?" I asked.

"I'm Virginia from the neurosurgery department."

"Oh, Virginia, is it true there really is a Santa Claus?" I quipped, recalling that line from an old Christmas movie.

"If you want there to be," she said. "Can I come in?"

"Sure. Are you a doctor?"

"No, I'm the Nurse Coordinator for the Department of Neurosurgery. I think you met Dr. Dacey, the head of the department yesterday. I work with him. I took the call from Emory and worked on getting you admitted, so I wanted to come up and check on you. You've been through a lot. How are you feeling?" she said.

"Better today. I'm glad to be back in Saint Louis, but I'm getting tired of needles and other stuff. How long will I be in the hospital?"

"That's partly up to you. You suffered a pretty bad injury only eleven days ago, so be patient. You need to do some healing, but your stay doesn't have to be too long."

It became quickly apparent that she wasn't an admissions person but a medical professional.

"What will I be doing next?" I asked.

"We're working on that. You just got here yesterday, so give us a little time to figure it out," she said. "Did you know that you're checked in and registered as patient X?" she asked.

"No. What does that mean?"

"Yours has been a pretty big news story. The press are all trying to get an interview and find out information about your condition. But don't worry, we'll keep them away," she said.

"Good," I said. I didn't realize that the shooting had been a big news story in both Saint Louis and Atlanta.

Virginia continued to check in on me daily, and she was the first to hear many of my questions about my prognosis. I continually asked her when I could go home. Her honest, even-keeled responses were exactly what I needed. She never offered me false hope, but she made a point to encourage me. In addition to being a cheerful visitor, she quickly became a trusted voice.

I rapidly fell into a comfortable routine at Barnes, accepting visitors and trying to be a good patient. I had not eaten well in Atlanta, and one friend asked if he could bring me anything special.

"A bag of White Castle hamburgers and a beer," I answered.

When he brought both, I rediscovered my appetite.

Dr. Dacey and the other neurosurgery doctors checked in on me daily, and the floor nurses made me feel like I was their favorite patient. I'm sure it wasn't true, but that speaks to the skill and professionalism of these hard workers. I remained on antiseizure and anti-brain-swelling medications delivered intravenously, so I had an IV line in twenty-four seven. This became the bane of my existence as the heparin lock, which was supposed to stay in place for days, came out of my arm at least once a day, which meant the device had to be reinserted. Some of the nurses were quite good and could hit my vein on the first try, but others—especially in the middle of the night—couldn't hit a vein in four or five attempts. These are among my most painful memories. After several failed attempts, I'd finally say, "Get the stick team." I needed the group that sets IV needles as a specialty.

Day by day, I gradually became more alert. While I still napped, I was always happy to receive visitors. I'm sure my visitors must have been filled with trepidation to see me in such a condition, but they all put up a cheery and positive front. There were even glimpses of how we used to have fun at one another's expense.

Gary, my friend since high school, visited. "Good thing I knew your room number, Mr. X," he said. "I tried to confirm your room number at the reception desk, and they said they didn't have a patient named Bill Johnson." As we talked, he mentioned that he'd gone to the airport to pick up my van from the short-term parking lot. I'd totally forgotten about my van.

"Your mom called and asked me to go get it. Of course, I didn't know where it was, so I had to work with airport security to locate it."

Don, the friend I'd called from Atlanta, and his wife Peggy visited too. Peggy immediately greeted me with, "Bill, all your hair turned grey!"

"Really?" I asked. I really wanted to be able to look in a mirror to see if she was telling the truth. Could the trauma have caused me to go grey overnight?

"Oh, I'm so sorry. You can't see," she teased.

Nobody would give me a straight answer about whether or not I had a head full of grey hair. But I would've been disappointed if this gang hadn't given me a hard time. I was still the same person, and I wanted them to treat me that way. Their teasing was another glimpse of my old life and relationships, and I was glad that everything didn't have to change. If I just kept putting one foot in front of the other, all would be well and life would go on.

I had some really long days in the hospital, and while I was still in Atlanta, my sister had given me a cassette player and a couple of music tapes—Fine Young Cannibals and 10,000 Maniacs. Being a classic rock fan, I questioned her taste, but I learned to enjoy both. Others in Saint Louis thoughtfully brought me books on tape—*The Hitchhiker's*

Guide to the Galaxy and *When Bad Things Happen to Good People*, which was the shorter one, so I listened to it first. The book described what had already been my natural reaction to what I'd experienced: Don't ask God "Why has this happened to me?" but ask "Now that this has happened, what should I do next?" I'd never read pop psychology or self-help books, and I didn't have enough belief to have blamed God, but the message reverberated deeply with me. It supported my natural inclination to go on with life.

"Now that this has happened, what should I do next?" The answer was to do the next right thing. The message was clear. I needed to get out of the hospital and get on with learning to live, work, and help raise my children as a blind person. I didn't have a template for how to do any of this, but I had a sense of urgency to get on with it.

———

The phone rang in my hospital room and I picked it up.

"Bill?" I heard in a stern, distinctive voice.

"Ben. How are you?" I asked. It was a neighbor from the lake. When we had bought our lake house in the early 1980s, Ben was our neighbor three houses away. He and his wife Doris had raised three sons in Kansas City, and they were now retired and living full time at the lake. Ben was a unique lake character and a good friend. He tried to fix everything with baling wire, duct tape, and a long screw, and he was always willing to help us "city kids," as he affectionately called us. He was still slalom skiing at the age of sixty-five and would reach down to grab the ski he was dropping, then ski around with it under his arm. He often came over in his very classic, old Correct Craft boat to socialize.

"How are you feeling?" he asked.

"OK," I answered. "They're taking good care of me, but I missed getting down there for the Fourth of July."

"Listen to me," he said, abruptly. "If this thing ever gets you down, don't do anything—but call me. Will you promise me that?"

"Yes, sure Ben," I said, not really grasping his meaning.

"I'm serious. Do you promise?"

"Yes. Now, how is Doris? Did you have a big crowd at your place for the Fourth?" I asked.

Reflecting on the call, I remembered that one of his sons had been paralyzed in a kitesurfing accident at the lake. He never found peace with it and had taken his own life just before we met Ben, around ten years ago. Now I understood the reason for his call, and I was touched that he cared enough about me to bring it up.

My mind was starting to perk up, and that afternoon I had some questions I wanted to ask Katherine.

"How did you hear about what had happened?"

"Tuesday night I got home late from work," she said. Katherine worked for a large law firm in Chicago. "The phone was ringing, and it was Mom. She told me there'd been a shooting in Atlanta, and that you and two others had been shot. She said that Keith had been killed, Tony was in critical condition, and your injuries were severe, but less life threatening."

"Nice call to get, eh?" I joked.

"It was terrible, but it was worse for Mom and Dad. The police had called them, and then their phone started ringing with calls from news reporters."

"What did you do next?"

"Mom said you'd been 'shot in the face' and that Dad had already flown to Atlanta. She said she'd keep me posted.

"I talked to some friends, and we all agreed that you might recover from a shot to the face but would probably have some disfigurement. Thank God you weren't shot straight on, like I'd pictured.

"We didn't know if you'd be home in a couple of days, a couple of weeks, or never. We talked to Dad in Atlanta. He told us that you had been taken to the ER, had a straight-forward surgery, and were currently heavily sedated. The doctor said the real concern was your eyesight. I decided to fly to Atlanta as soon as possible and made a 6:00 A.M. flight the next morning."

"That was quick," I said, grasping the urgency they had felt.

"I met Dad at the Ritz. He said KPMG had insisted that he move there from the Holiday Inn and that they'd pick up the bill. I quickly figured out that we were celebrities. You can't imagine how big of a news story this was in Atlanta. The town was horrified that this could have happened there. When Dad and I got off the elevator at Grady Memorial Hospital, we were met by Rich, the man from KPMG whom you met. He was turning away the press and mis-guided well-wishers that wanted to see you."

Starting to get a sense of the scene, I joked, "Stick with me and you'll be famous."

"Finally, they let us in to see you. You looked terri-ble." Here, Katherine paused. "Do you want to know the details?"

"Sure."

"I think I told you a little of this in Atlanta, but since you look almost normal now, I can tell you this. You were rest-ing on a hospital bed, wearing a large, diaper-like garment. You looked very swollen and badly injured. The craniotomy incision was held together with very angry-looking staples, and the entry and exit wounds at your temples were very visible. It was extremely upsetting, especially to Dad.

"Sounds ugly. What did you do?" I asked.

"The staff suggested we try to communicate with you, so we talked a lot and squeezed your hand. At first, you didn't respond at all, but later you were able to squeeze our hands back. The really awful thing was that Tony was in the same ICU with you. He looked fine, but we heard that he was on life support, waiting for his family to gather."

I was surprised to hear that Tony and I'd been in the same room, but I hadn't been aware of anything at that time.

"When Dad and I left that first day, he just kept saying, 'damn it,' over and over and over again. I've never seen him in tears, but he was close."

Now that I was back in Saint Louis, it came time to see my kids, and Laura, my ex-wife, brought them to visit. They were five and six years old, and we'd given much thought about how and when to let them see me. They knew that I'd been shot and was now blind, but we were concerned that seeing me all beat up could traumatize them. My sister Katherine wanted to see them, too, so she made a point to be there.

While I was in the hospital in Atlanta, Kelly had celebrated her fifth birthday on July seventh. I hated to miss it.

"Come over here and see me, birthday girl," I said to Kelly.

She quickly scrambled up on the bed. "Hi Dad. Now can we get a seeing eye dog?" She was way ahead of me on looking for a silver lining.

Chris was a little more reticent. Assuming he was there, I said, "Chris, how are you?"

"OK, I guess. Are you OK?"

"I'll be fine. It will just take me a little while."

Although I couldn't see their faces, I could hold their little bodies and hear their voices. They were still the same. I was still the same. I was still their dad.

The days passed, and my treatment team was wrestling with where to send me for blindness rehabilitation. It was obvious that I wouldn't have any lasting physical or medical injuries from the shooting, and the staff was a bit perplexed about how to address my instant blindness. The social services worker referred me to the Saint Louis Society for the Blind and arranged for one of their counselors to visit.

Doris Westfall explained who the organization served. "Generally, it's people who have age-related loss of vision."

I clearly wasn't in that group, so she suggested that I reach out to the State of Missouri Department of Rehabilitation Services for the Blind.

"They're more oriented to helping people gain skills to return to work and holistic blindness rehabilitation," she said.

"Based on your experience, do you think I'm crazy to expect to go back to my old job?" I asked.

"The way you describe it, I don't know why you shouldn't," she said. "There are a number of blind people in Saint Louis who work for some of the largest companies, like Southwestern Bell, Monsanto, and Anheuser Busch. Why shouldn't you join them?"

"That's good to know. I guess I'll need to learn a few things before I can do that," I said.

"Yes, and the State of Missouri should be your key," she said.

Doris made the referral call before she left and promised that someone would contact me shortly after I got home.

Amidst all the seriousness of my situation, many things struck me as funny from day one. The people who delivered my meals had been trained to tell me where all the food was on my plate: Eggs at five o'clock, toast at nine o'clock, yogurt at twelve o'clock, etc. The only problem was that they were standing at the foot of my bed when they described the contents of my tray. Their clock was upside down, and invariably they gave me totally incorrect information. At this point I was "seeing" most of my food by feeling it with my fingers and eating with them as well. It really didn't matter if they told me where things were or not.

CHAPTER
FOUR

Admitting that I was now blind was simple. After all, I was in a hospital room, could see only blackness, had knocked over several drinks, and when I was finally free of the IV lines, I was still not allowed to get out of bed by myself. But *admitting* the fact was quite different from *accepting* what had happened to me.

When I'd regained consciousness in Atlanta, my first reaction was, *What's the big deal?* and then, *Get me out of here.* I didn't want to be a needy patient. I knew I was the same person that I'd been a week earlier. I had the same memories, wanted to do the same things, and was quite willing to overlook the fact that being blind might cause major changes in my life. My reaction was equal parts denial and male macho, thinking I can do anything without taking the slightest glance at what those things entailed.

I told anyone who would listen, "Just let me out of here, so I can go back to my house, my job, and my life." That became my mantra. That reaction was obviously contrary to the facts that the logical part of me should have inventoried. It came from the emotional, subconscious me that—in spite of the evidence—held on to the possibility that this was all a dream or that a miracle would occur and I would see again.

That initial bluster and denial served a purpose. It allowed me to assimilate all the information I could about my changed circumstances in order to deal with them in the best way I could. It was an instinctual, irrational reaction, but as long as that denial thrived, I couldn't truly accept my situation and engage in the fight to regain my life.

Denial is not a loner; it travels with its close companion, delusion. The delusion was that my new situation was just a dream. That I would wake up the next day and open my eyes to light, familiar faces, and all the richness and surprise of the world I was used to seeing. Or that an operation would reverse the blindness. Couldn't doctors do almost anything?

To accept my new reality, I had to be fearlessly honest about my situation, which didn't come naturally. When confronted with a choice between doing the responsible thing or the fun thing, I normally chose the fun thing. I tended to avoid tough decisions until the last minute, procrastinated about starting large undertakings, and generally looked for the softer, gentler approach as long as I could.

For over two weeks I'd lain in bed while others waited on me. All my basic needs had been fulfilled. Very little effort—and no thinking—had been required of me. I simply flirted with the nurses and presented a positive face to my friends and family.

As I was migrated from IV drugs to pills, I was given a release date that I had to face. The real world loomed ahead of me. My parents still wanted me to move in with them, but the thought of being mothered at the age of forty-one still didn't appeal to me, and I stuck to my guns. I was going home.

When some of the medical devices were finally removed and I needed less frequent medical attention, I had more time to myself. One quiet afternoon at Barnes, I thought about how all I could see was blackness. Then that thought grabbed me: *I will never see anything again.* Could I handle this, live a life steeped in darkness? The boring black of my reality consumed me, overwhelmed me. All those happy thoughts of going home, the stiff upper lip, and my cheerful attitude were whisked away. I repeated to myself, "I will never see again."

The truth hit me really hard. No denial. No deluding myself about my new reality. *I can't just open my eyes to end this*, I thought. Sweat broke out across my forehead and a single drop rolled down the side of my face. There was no escape.

In high school, I'd gone on a spelunking trip with my good friend, Gary, and some others I didn't know so well. One of them knew about a cave on the Meramec River that had a tight passage that opened up into a large underground room. Sounded like fun, so off we went. We followed his directions and arrived at the river.

"It should be just down river a bit, then up on the hill."

We walked up the gravel bar and looked around the surrounding hills and bluffs for a cave.

"There's one!" someone hollered.

"That looks like it," Gary's friend said.

We climbed up to the cave opening and plunged from the sun into the cool, dark cave. We each had wildly different experiences in caves, none of it great, and scant equipment—only a couple of helmet-mounted carbide lamps. I had explored a couple of caves before with my Explorer Post, and since I'd brought my carbide lamp that was screwed to a construction helmet, I became the leader.

A carbide lamp is what miners use. It has an upper chamber that holds water and a lower chamber that holds calcium carbide. As the water drips into the lower chamber, it produces acetylene, which flows to the center of the reflector. When the lamp is ignited, it produces a steady flame to light the way.

I filled my carbide light with river water to start the chemical reaction, spun the sparker, and my light came to life. *Pss sssss pssss hssss!* The light spit as I heard the flame at my forehead burn.

The cave we'd looked for had a medium-sized room that connected to a very large underground cavern via a long, low tunnel.

"This looks like the first part of the cave," the guy said. "We need to find the low opening."

We stayed close together and inspected all the cave walls for openings.

"Over here!" one guy said, pointing to a low opening with water running out of it.

"That's it!"

I went in first. Initially, I could walk if I hunched over. My boots splashed in the water. The further in I went, the more my helmet hit the roof. The path got shorter and shorter, until I was forced to get on my hands and knees to continue. The bottom of the stream was soft with very damp Missouri clay, and every once in a while, my knee landed on a sharp rock.

Eventually, I was crawling on my stomach. I kept moving forward, thinking we had to be just a few feet from breaking into the large cavern. My clothes were soaked from the creek, and I was chilled in the cool cave air. Finally, I could go no further. The cave walls touched my back and both sides, and I was lying on my stomach with my hands in front of me. If I lifted my head to shine the light, I could see about fifteen feet. The space continued to shrink.

Just then, the guy behind me bumped into my feet. I hollered, "I can't go any further. Go back!"

"What?" his muffled voice said. I was facing away from him and my body plugged the space so tightly that I could barely hear him, and he couldn't hear me. *I can't go forward or back,* I thought, *and I can't tell them to back out.* I was terrified.

I scrunched up to one side of the space to let as much sound through as possible, but I could only create an opening of no more than an inch. "Turn back!" I hollered at the top of my lungs as my words rushed out ahead of me, not behind.

"Did you say turn back?" I heard.

"Yes. Yes! Turn back!"

He finally understood, but he had to get the message to the guy behind him, then the guy behind him, all the way down to the last man. Then we could start backing out.

Just then, my light sputtered out. I hadn't kept my carbide light level enough. I was surrounded by the most total darkness I'd ever know. Totally black. Completely cold. Terrifying. I lifted up my head, spun the striker again, and prayed that it would light. *Pfft hsssss hsssss.* Success!

It took several minutes for my friends to get the message down the line and to start backing out. I wondered if the earth could settle and close little slices below ground, like where we were. The walls and ceiling closed in even further, and I felt an overwhelming terror rise up in me. I wanted to get up and run, but I couldn't move. I wanted to freak out, scream, back into the guy behind me, push the earth above me to create some space, do anything but lie there quietly waiting for the guy behind me to move. But I stayed quiet. None of those reactions could help the situation. I needed to remain patient and calm, to surrender to the circumstance. I forced myself to lie calmly, trusting that my friends were backing out and that my turn would soon come. But the cold water kept running under my soaked clothes. I was totally powerless and feared I would never again see the light of day.

I felt a tap on my boots, and a muffled voice that said, "Bill, come on back." Just pushing myself backward with my hands and feeling the ceiling and side walls slowly move away from me was a relief. When I could finally turn around and crawl forward the rest of the way, my relief was total. We soon burst out into the pure joy of the warm, bright sun; we had made it out!

That afternoon in the hospital, I felt exactly like I had in the cave: terror-struck and helpless. Abject loneliness consumed me. I felt the terror of never again being able to see. Rather than scream, I again surrendered to the reality of my situation.

I don't know how much time passed, but eventually the bad feelings broke, and I experienced an overwhelming sense of contentment and peace of mind. I was infused with a powerful, undeniable belief that everything would be alright and that I could handle whatever was to come. My fears were completely removed.

That day in the hospital room, blindness confronted me head on. It forced out that last bit of denial and the delusion that accompanied it. I had only two choices: to stare my blindness in the face and do what I had to do to regain my life, or to be dependent on others for the rest of my life.

I lay in my bed and grinned. What had come over me to cause such total acceptance and peace? There had been many miracles in the past weeks, and this overwhelming peace was yet another. It was a miracle that I wasn't killed with my associates, a miracle that Grady Memorial Hospital was a world-renowned trauma hospital, and now the greatest miracle of all: the gift of acceptance was bestowed on me that afternoon in Barnes Hospital.

CHAPTER
FIVE

Of course, I'd never been blind before or had any other disabilities. Further, I'd had limited interaction with people who had disabilities, particularly the sensory types—those who were blind or deaf. I'd never been in situations that fostered close contact with them. Had I shied away from opportunities to approach people with disabilities and to get to know them as individuals? Sadly, probably yes.

Now I was looking at life from their perspective. I knew I was the same person with the same sense of humor, the same skills and knowledge, the same friends and family to support me, and all I wanted was for everyone to treat me the same way they would have a month ago—not as a blind man. I was still everything else I'd ever been; I just couldn't see.

I was vaguely aware of the political correctness regarding how people referred to those with disabilities. Many of my visitors seemed unsure of whether, or how, to reference my blindness. They said things like, "Your vision was affected," or, "Your vision problem," or they used the term *unsighted*, always with an uncomfortable tone in their voices. If someone said, "Hey Bill, did you see the . . ." it was quickly followed by, "Sorry."

My new circumstances were an obvious topic of interest and conversation. My friends and family hadn't necessarily had any more contact with people with disabilities than I had, and they didn't know what to say or how to say it. I sensed that they were afraid of saying something that would upset me, and their general discomfort was unsettling to me.

I needed to decide how I would refer to myself, so others could follow my lead. I should be the one to show my family and friends the way. If I was comfortable with certain terms, then others would be too. I knew that people were referred to as handicapped, disabled, other-abled, and maybe more. *Other-abled* seemed like venturing so far into political correctness that the term didn't have any actual meaning. I knew that *handicapped* carried some connotation of being limited in some ways and was considered to be offensive and not politically correct. I thought *disabled* sounded about right PC-wise, but that word didn't really describe me.

Was I visually impaired? Were there other softer sounding terms that described my new situation? Initially, the word *blind* sounded very harsh. It took no prisoners and was so final.

Early on, the doctors got around having to choose a term by saying, "There may be some chance that your vision will return to some degree, but there's no way to know whether you'll regain any functional vision." What in the world did that mean? Was it their way to avoid using that harsh term and giving me a final prognosis? It was confusing.

From the beginning, whenever anyone mentioned, "your lack of vision," or, "your inability to see," I followed up with a sentence using the word *blind* as I referenced myself. It sounded harsh to me, and I'm sure it did to my friends and family, but it also felt right.

I was blind.

It was important to deal with truth head on. No political correctness, no sugar coating. And no hanging on to the faint hope that some doctors held out that when the swelling in my head went down, pressure on the optic nerves might be relieved, and some vision could be restored. Perhaps they were taking a softer position with me, not to encourage me, but to present it as a remote possibility. But I heard it as hope offered.

One day a neuro ophthalmologist, Dr. Debra Barrett visited me. "You've had quite an experience," she said. "How are you feeling now?"

"OK. Especially now that I'm in Saint Louis and get to see my friends."

"I'd like to take a quick look at you now and then schedule an appointment for you to come to my office before you're released. I've got a tool that lets me look at the inside of your eyes, so try not to blink as I look into each one."

"Sure." By this time, the pain in my eyes was minimal, and the blackout glasses were gone.

"Left eye first," she said as she held my head steady.

After looking in both eyes, she said "There's definitely retina damage. I want to see you in my office to get a better look. I'll schedule it for tomorrow."

The next day I was taken to her office in a wheelchair. I sat in the examining chair while she looked into my eyes with various devices. She asked if the residents in training could come in and do the same. I believe the teaching topic was what a doctor sees when looking into eyes that can't see. A number of the residents took turns examining me.

"Hmmmmm."

"Hello, Sir."

"Oooo," another one commented.

Responding to a question, I said, "I can see a small bit of light." Given what they saw in the interior of my eyes, Dr. Barrett didn't believe me. She turned off all of the lights in the examining room.

"I have a pen light with a silent off/on switch. Tell me when the light turns on or off," she said.

"Off."

"On."

"Off."

"On," I said as I perceived the smallest bit of light. She then asked me to close one eye and then the other, so she could determine which eye had the bit of light perception.

I convinced her that I wasn't guessing or hearing the click of her silent pen light, but that I really did see a little light through my right eye.

"You'll probably never read the New York Times," she said but indicated that I might regain some vision. She then suggested, "You should go out and get the best looking, most expensive sunglasses you can find."

Quite a mixed message. Rather than being encouraged, I believed that she—and others—simply weren't comfortable telling me straight out that I would be forever blind. It's fine to be optimistic, but I knew deep down that my vision would never improve. Her sunglasses joke confirmed it; she had lumped me in with Ray Charles, Stevie Wonder, and Ronnie Millsap.

—————■—————

I woke up to a voice in my room. "Good morning, Mr. Johnson. Today, you're scheduled for your first physical therapy session," the nurse said.

"What? Why physical therapy?" I asked.

"You've been lying in bed for weeks now, and we have to be careful about getting you back on your feet."

I thought that was preposterous but welcomed this chance to get out of bed for the first time.

"I'm going to remove this drip, so you can work with the physical therapist without the IV."

Ah, freedom! I'd been tethered to a tube or device since the shooting, and the idea of freedom of movement sounded good.

Ten minutes later, I heard a knock on the door.

"Who is it?"

"Hi. I'm Sue from Physical Therapy," the pleasant voice answered.

"OK. You're not going to torture me, are you?"

"We'll see how you do, but we try not to torture anyone," she said. "I've looked over your records. Can you see anything at all?"

"No."

"Have you been out of bed yet?"

"Only twice—to get an MRI and to visit the neuro ophthalmologist, but I was in a wheelchair both times."

"I want to get you on your feet. Then we can go upstairs to the physical therapy department. Can you get out of bed?" she asked as she lowered the rail on one side of my bed.

"We'll find out," I said, swinging my legs off the bed and feeling for the floor.

"Be careful," she said, as she and another nurse grabbed my arms. "How does that feel?"

"OK." I was weaker than I thought.

"Can you steady yourself on me, and we'll walk to the elevator?"

"Sure."

Together, we walked awkwardly to the elevator. At one point she said, "Walk this way."

Ever the joker, I responded, "Who do you give the most credit for that song? *Run*-D.M.C. or Arrowsmith?" Being

much younger, she didn't get my decade-old music reference, but at least I thought it was clever.

"How does walking feel?" Sue asked.

"My legs really hurt. Like maybe my hamstrings," I
said.

"You've been lying down for a long time, so that's understandable. We need to stretch out your muscles."

We tried to climb some stairs, but I could barely go up
them. After several sessions of PT, it was better, and before
long I was sneaking from my hospital bed to the bathroom.

Of course, I'd been instructed to call for a bedpan
whenever I needed to use the bathroom, but I'd had enough
of that.

The first trip from bed to bathroom was a little scary,
but it was also exhilarating. Fortunately, I was familiar with
hospital room configurations from visiting patients, plus I'd
professionally consulted with several hospitals about telecommunications challenges between nurses, doctors, patients, and nurses stations. From the knocking sounds on
my door and the voices of people that entered, I pictured
the door being on the wall to my right, at the far end of the
wall at my feet. I figured the bathroom should be against the
same wall, but inside and to the left as you entered the room.

I used my hand to trace down to the foot of my bed,
along the wall toward the door, and back across the room
where I thought the bathroom should be. My guess was correct, and I got a kick out of my first taste of independence.

After several sessions, Sue said, "Next time I see you,
we'll go to your house. Peggy, the occupational therapist
you met, wants to take a look at it and observe how well
you get around." And, I was sure, to decide if it was wise
to let this single blind man out of the hospital to go live by
himself.

"That will be great," I answered.

It felt like a test, and I was committed to impressing Peggy and Sue with my ability to navigate around my own home. I began to visualize my house, and studied in my head what I would do. I thought about the layout. I owned a small ranch house and couldn't imagine where I could possibly have a problem.

When it was time to go, a nurse took me downstairs in a wheelchair, where Peggy and Sue were waiting for me in Peggy's car.

"Stand up, Mr. Johnson," the nurse said. "I'll get the car door for you. Here, feel the door? Watch your head."

"Thanks," I said as I slid into the seat.

"Enjoy your visit," she said, and off we went.

As we drove, I felt the last several turns and tried to guess where we were. We bumped up the slight curb into my driveway and stopped. "Here we are," Peggy said.

I jumped out of the car and felt for the handrail. Found it. There were steps that led from the driveway to an elevated front porch and the front door. I quickly headed up the stairs, using the hand rail. "Slow down," Peggy suggested.

"I'm going to unlock the door," I said, as I felt for the lock. I got my key, felt for the rough side, and inserted the key with the rough side up. Turning the key, I opened the door to my house. Finally, I was making progress back to my life!

I cruised around the house like I'd been doing this all my life. It seemed natural to run my hand along the front of my fish tank as I walked by. Then I turned right toward my bedroom and dragged a finger along the wall for orientation. In the hospital, I'd either held onto someone else or walked with my hands straight out in front of me, Frankenstein-style. This was more natural. I could picture the layout of my house and its furnishings in my mind, and I knew I could move around safely.

"There's my bedroom, and the bathroom is right here."

"Good," Peggy said.

I backtracked with my left finger tracing down the hall, then moved across a short open space, avoiding the dining room table and chairs, until I arrived at another wall. I turned right and felt with my left hand until I came to the kitchen door.

"The kitchen," I said proudly.

"What's this door all about?" she asked.

"You mean the glass door that goes nowhere?"

"Yes. It looks dangerous. Did you know that it drops off ten feet right outside that door?"

"Yes," I said. "I was just getting ready to build a new deck. I put that door in to access the deck as I built it, but I haven't started the construction yet. I guess I'll have to hire a contractor to do it."

"That worries me," she said. "Are you sure you won't get confused and try to walk out that door? You could really hurt yourself."

"No way. I promise. I've never used that door other than when I installed it."

I went back toward the front door and perched on the arm of a sofa.

"Be careful," Peggy said.

"I'm OK. Did I pass the test? Do I get to come home?"

"Yes. I guess so," she answered.

On the way out, just for good measure, I showed off by leaning over the porch rail, sitting on the porch swing, and following the shrubbery from the front walk to the street. It felt great to feel these familiar things, to have a taste of my independent life again.

Within a day or two, I had my release date. I woke up early that morning. After breakfast, Virginia came to take the staples out of my scalp. She helped me out of bed and over to a chair. She used a tool to remove the staples, but the pain and the sound reverberating in my head was excruciating. It was like pulling nails out of a two-by-four with a claw hammer.

"EEEEEOwww!" I screamed. There were a lot of staples, and I was almost in tears by the time she finished. The pain was even worse than re-setting my IV at 3:00 a.m.

"Don't be a sissy," Virginia teased. "They're just in the skin."

Now that I was unstapled, it was time to fly.

CHAPTER
SIX

During college, I'd worked summers at Southwestern Bell, performing a variety of technical and office jobs: station installer, lineman, frame man, mail room clerk, and office intern. I understood how traditional telephony worked and had applied for a job with the telephone company when I completed my MBA. I thought my hands-on summer experience in conjunction with my MBA made me a perfect hire. For a variety of reasons, including my grades, no offer was extended, and I ended up working for Chrysler as a factory dealer rep in southern Illinois.

That was not my ideal job, so soon after, I joined a couple of high school friends who sold advertising specialties and premiums. Trinkets and promotional swag. For me, it was mostly an opportunity to go back to a college student lifestyle. We did a lot of partying but also a lot of very creative strategizing for our clients, actual and potential. It was great fun, and it would have been interesting if we were actually making a reasonable amount of money.

It was time to look for a real job, even though I hadn't added much to my resume since getting out of school. Fortunately, Southwestern Bell was ramping up their business marketing department in reaction to the emerging competition of the 1970's, and they hired me.

About a year later, I started dating an attractive and interesting girl who was one of the secretaries for our group.

We were thrown together by several other employees at a happy hour, and one thing led to another. It was kind of a whirlwind and was exciting for a couple of months. We hid our relationship at work but saw a lot of each other after hours.

Within a couple of months, I was called in to see my boss's boss. This had never happened before, so I wondered if I was in trouble. Maybe it was about dating Laura? But, no. He told me what a good job I'd been doing and described a relatively untapped market for Southwestern Bell in Arkansas. He offered me a promotion to serve that territory, which meant a move to Little Rock. Turning down a promotion was career suicide, so I said, "Thank you very much. I appreciate the opportunity and your confidence in me." That decision changed my life in many ways.

For a number of reasons, Laura and I decided that we should get married immediately and move to Arkansas, even though we'd only been dating for a couple of months. It was a chaotic time. Too many things going on and such big decisions to make.

We had a large wedding followed by a honeymoon in Jamaica. It was all very exciting and new. In many ways, we were still getting to know each other.

When we arrived in Arkansas, we learned that we were Yankees. Being from Saint Louis, I'd never identified with either side in the Civil War. In Arkansas, being called a Yankee wasn't a compliment, nor was it an insult. It was just a statement that we were different from the others. They thought Saint Louis was a big city and questioned why anyone would want to live there. I often stood up for Saint Louis by explaining that we didn't live in the whole metropolitan area, but usually lived, shopped, and worked in a small area. In Little Rock, there was only one of everything, but the different places you had to go were spread out across the whole town. We spent as much time driving around in Little Rock as we had in Saint Louis.

As newlyweds, we were thrown into this new place where we were different, had no friends, and were still getting to know each other. Laura also worked at Southwestern Bell, so we saw each other at work and at home. Friendships came slowly.

Over time, we did make some friends. We both pursued our careers, and Laura was promoted, as was I. We bought a ski boat and enjoyed the lakes around Little Rock. But we ignored the fact that we didn't have much fun when we spent time alone.

After three and a half years, the Bell System was being deregulated, and it looked like we might be in Little Rock for a long time. AT&T was being broken into two separate companies, and Southwestern Bell was becoming an independent entity. Each of the three separate companies would have well-defined portions of the telecommunications market, and we were all asked to select which company we wanted to work for. In the midst of this chaos, I was offered an opportunity to move back to Saint Louis with Southwestern Bell. That made my choice easy, and Laura and I moved back home.

Laura transferred to AT&T in Saint Louis. Within a few years we added two kids to the family, our son Chris and our daughter Kelly.

Our marriage had had some rocky spots, and, unfortunately, our differences soon became too big to resolve. When Kelly was three and a half, Laura announced that she wanted a divorce. I give her credit for having the backbone and courage to make that decision.

The divorce started out as fairly business-like. We even met with a mediator in hopes that it could be finalized quickly. But that wasn't to be. Before long, the lawyers were delaying things, and we were in court for temporary visitation schedules, etc. Money was never the issue, but child custody and visitation were hot points. I felt that my time with my kids, and therefore our relationship, had been severely threatened for the two years it took to finalize the divorce. In the end, I was awarded the standard visitation schedule, which was all I'd wanted to begin with.

Meanwhile, my professional life had progressed. With the break-up of the Bell System, many outside opportunities had been created in the market, and I was offered a job to become a telecommunications consultant at Coopers & Lybrand, one of the "Big 8" accounting and consulting firms. I didn't think my career was going anywhere at Southwestern Bell, and the division I was in was experiencing growing pains, so I accepted the offer.

I had a broad background in the telecommunications business, but I wasn't really prepared to be, in essence, the entire telecommunications consulting department. The man who'd hired me quit, and I had no other support staff to rely upon. I was responsible to sell enough consulting work to create a profit center, to deliver that consulting work, and to make sure the clients were pleased enough to pay their bills.

I had a pretty steep learning curve during this period with pressure to sell work, deliver work, and hire staff to work for me. For the first six months I often thought, *I quit a good job to do this. Am I crazy?* But before too long, I landed some large projects around Saint Louis. The work was all delivered successfully; the clients all paid their bills. And I enjoyed the consulting role.

I never really got the hang of hiring and training staff, so I was stuck in a cycle of selling, then delivering all my own work. When one project ended, I might be unbillable until I sold the next project. We called this "shoot it, skin it, and eat it," and it wasn't an approach that had a future. I was surviving, but it was stressful. It was a nice paycheck, and I came to really like the work, but it didn't have much future unless I hired and built a staff of ten to twelve people. I was a little wary of going down that road with my niche expertise in telecommunications (soon to be reborn as networking and telecommunications), compared to my coworkers who were mostly working with large computing applications.

By 1988, I'd caught the attention of another consulting firm, Peat Marwick Mitchell. Tony Lake was a senior manager in Saint Louis in the telecommunications consulting practice. He was more politically adept than I and was in the process of being promoted to partner. He was building the staff under him, and he approached me about teaming up. It seemed like a great idea. Tony had a degree in computer science from MIT and was very knowledgeable about telecommunications and networking theory and strategy. I had much more practical experience in designing, specifying, and acquiring systems that worked for my clients. We had an immediate understanding of our complementary strengths.

Peat Marwick was a larger firm than Coopers & Lybrand, and I felt that the jobs I'd previously held had taken me from a paycheck to a professional career. I liked everything and everyone I'd met at Peat Marwick. It was a great opportunity, and I accepted their offer about six months before my marriage broke up.

Within a couple of years, Tony's responsibilities expanded to cover the upper Midwest, and his group took on security and data center work, in addition to networking and telecommunications. Tony asked me to lead the networking and telecom part of his practice.

We had staff in Saint Louis, Chicago, and Minneapolis. The whole group was around twenty strong, and it appeared that my career was really taking off. In the summer of 1991, Tony told me that my name would be on the partner candidate list the following year. With his support, and the continued growth of our practice, I had a chance to make it to the next level. Finally, I'd arrived where I wanted to be with my career. My varied background and job experiences had all contributed to my ability to function in this environment. I'd earned a leadership position and was part of a team that provided quality work for our clients. There was even an expectation that we could eventually centralize the practice for the entire country in Saint Louis.

Professionally things were looking good, but personally, the divorce had taken a large emotional toll. There was constant disagreement about everything. Even after the divorce was final, we couldn't agree on the summer visitation schedule. Paying child support on top of maintaining my own home put some financial stress in my life, but I just kept going forward. I knew that if I kept paying attention to my work and made every effort to make the time with my kids quality time, I was doing what I needed to do.

I lived a hectic life during this period, traveling out of town most weeks. Weekends were spent with my kids or at the lake. I never slowed down and never thought of my situation as much different than many other guys' my age: a divorced working father moving on to the next chapter of my life.

In early July 1991, Tony and I'd flown to Atlanta for a quick meeting with Keith Jonas, a client who was head of IT at C&S Sovran Bank. We had an ongoing consulting project with them, but this meeting was primarily to strategize with Keith. There were rumors that NationsBank was considering a takeover of C&S Sovran. We had first met Keith when he worked at Sovran, which was acquired by Citizens and Southern Bank in Atlanta. Keith was able to advance his career in the combined companies, even though he came from the acquired bank. He hoped to be able to do the same thing if the NationsBank rumors were true, and he asked us to help him prepare.

We'd flown in on Sunday night, strategized Monday and Tuesday, and were to fly out on Tuesday afternoon.

Tuesday morning, Tony asked, "Keith, can your secretary call us a cab for the airport?"

"Why don't you just take MARTA?" he said. "It's only a few blocks away, and the weather's great. You'll get to the airport faster than a cab. I'll walk with you. We can finish our discussion, and I can get some air."

We'd been meeting at a support location on the fringe of downtown. The neighborhood was a little sketchy, and Keith took us on a shortcut through a couple of alleys. Birds were looking for treats in the dumpsters, and the summer breezes swirled up random dust and scraps of paper. We emerged from the last alley just a block from the MARTA entrance.

"There's the station," Keith said as we made our way down the relatively empty sidewalk.

CHAPTER
SEVEN

The day had finally come. I'd been in three different hospitals, met numerous doctors and nurses, and had flown in an air ambulance—not to mention several rides in regular ambulances. All new experiences. I believed that because of my nagging, they'd moved me from Emory University Hospital in Atlanta to Saint Louis. And now I was getting what I really wanted. I was going home. In reality, my hospital stay probably wasn't reduced by even one day because of my efforts, but that's not what I thought at the time.

In the hospital, I'd been given almost no instruction about how to function as a blind person, and I'd had little opportunity to learn through trial and error. It was a very protected environment where nurses waited on me at all times. If I needed anything, I just hit the call button, and a nurse came to assist. My world consisted of two things: what I could feel (the hospital bed, the table that rolled over my lap, various tubes attached to my body); and the things I could hear (my telephone, a small radio, and the voices of friends and medical staff, who were all interested in me and how they could help).

I didn't know what I didn't know about the life that was to come. *What will I do at home?* I wondered. I was somewhat afraid of the unknown, but that was overshadowed by my belief that as I regained my old life, all would be OK. Going home was a big step.

It seemed like such a long time since I'd left for that quick trip to Atlanta, but it had only been three weeks. What a different person I was—or was I? I felt like the same person, and I never considered that I wouldn't be able to do anything I'd done before. I didn't think about the fact that I'd have to figure out new ways to do many things.

The morning of my departure, I took my first real shower.

"Don't get your head too wet or you'll risk opening one of the incisions," the nurse said. She handed me the clean clothes my parents had delivered for this day. I also had my shaving kit and decided that it would feel good to brush my teeth. I grabbed my toothpaste in one hand and my brush in the other, then poised over the sink.

"Ha, ha, ha," I laughed.

"What's so funny?" the nurse asked.

"How am I supposed to get the right amount of toothpaste on the brush without looking at it?"

"I don't know. You'll have to figure it out," she answered.

I did the only thing I could think of and raised the end of the tube to my mouth, squeezed the right amount onto my tongue, then put the brush in my mouth. Problem solved!

A little later, Virginia showed up again and saw me in street clothes for the first time. "You clean up pretty well, Mr. Johnson," she said.

"It felt good to take a shower," I said, doubting that my cut-up scalp and bad haircut looked very good.

"It's been great to have a patient with such a good attitude," she said. "I hope everything goes well for you at home."

"Thanks. I'm not sure what will happen when I get home, but I'm ready to find out."

"I've got some instructions for you," she continued. "Here's a supply of the medications you're still taking and a prescription for you to get more. You'll need to call our office if you have any problems or there are any changes in your condition. Make an appointment to be seen in our clinic in about a week."

"Who should I ask for when I call?"

"You can ask for me," she said. "I'll be able to answer your questions, or if I can't, I'll get you to the doctor."

"Thanks for all you've done for me, Virginia. Except maybe for taking out those staples. That really hurt."

Soon after, a nurse showed up with a wheelchair. "Are you ready to go?"

"Past ready!"

"I'll push you down to your dad's car."

"I can walk," I said.

"You probably can, but you have to leave the hospital in a wheelchair. Insurance and all. Your mom will be up in a minute, and your dad is waiting outside with the car, so please stand up."

"All right," I agreed. It didn't sound like walking out on my own power was negotiable.

"Turn around, and I'll push the chair up behind you. Then you can sit down."

Mom arrived and the nurse guided the wheelchair out of the hospital room. It felt good to be leaving it, never to return.

As we passed the nursing station, I heard many voices.

"Good luck, Mr. Johnson."

"Come back and tell us how everything is going."

"We enjoyed having you as a patient, Mr. Johnson."

"You guys were all fantastic," I answered. "Thanks for everything you did."

The wheelchair bumped on to the elevator. We exited on the first floor and went through the lobby and out into a warm Saint Louis morning. I heard horns honking and many people coming and going.

The nurse pushed the wheelchair to a curb and said, "Time to stand up," as she grabbed my arm. I heard a car door open. "Careful, careful," the nurse said. "Reach out. Do you feel the car door?"

"Yes."

"Follow along to the left of the door and find the seat."

"Got it," I said.

"Now get in. Watch your head," she said, and I felt her firm hand push my head under the opening of the door, as I sat on the seat.

Then we were off to the rest of my life.

I felt the car accelerate away from the curb and continue up to the stoplight at Kingshighway. Left on Kingshighway. The car turned, and my weight shifted to the right. I felt every bump in the road. On to the viaduct over the tracks, off the viaduct and up to the stop light. We turned right onto the entrance ramp up to I-44 toward home. I felt the sweeping turn over the River Des Peres, and pictured the big Laclede Gas storage tanks I'd often passed in Shrewsbury. Then we went down the exit ramp at Elm. Before long, I felt the bump as we turned right into my driveway and came to a stop. For the entire trip, I had visualized where we were.

Until now, I hadn't walked much on my own. I'd spent three weeks in a hospital bed, and with the exception of one quick home visit with the occupational therapist and a couple of PT sessions, I hadn't even left my hospital room. I'd been taught none of what I would come to learn as "daily living skills." I hadn't even been given a white cane, although that thought hadn't occurred to me yet. I was starting with zero adaptation skills.

Nevertheless, I was anxious to get out of the car. I felt for the hedge and followed it along the driveway to the steps. Right turn, and I found the wrought iron railing that led to the front porch. Up the steps, turn left, up more steps to the front door. All these things felt familiar and comfortable. For the last three weeks, nothing had felt familiar, but now this did. *I've got this down!* I thought to myself.

"I'll get your bags," Dad said.

Somehow, my suitcase and briefcase had made the journey back to Saint Louis with me—everything but my suit that had been cut off and my shoes. It felt good to unpack my suitcase. Dirty clothes went down the clothes chute, and my shaving kit went on the bathroom counter. Suitcase put away in the bottom of the closet. Perfect.

"What can we do for you?" Mom and Dad peppered me with questions, hoping to help. "What do you need?"

"What can I help you with?"

"Do you want me to show you where something is?"

"Do you need anything from the store?"

I had no idea what anyone could do for me, or even what I needed. I just wanted to be left alone to deal with things as they came up.

I gave Mom a list for the grocery store, and she seemed happy to be able to help. Dad and I sat in my living room. "Is there anything I can do for you?" he asked.

"I don't know. Let me look around here," I said.

I started feeling my way around my house. Going through this exercise helped me build a picture memory of the layout of my house and confirmed that things were in the same places I'd left them. Dining room table and chairs, living room sofa.

"Ouch!" I found the coffee table with my shin. Side table with a lamp on it. I continued. Opening drawers was much more of a challenge. The mail and bill drawer was a mystery. None of the paper in there meant a thing. *There's an issue to figure out*, I told myself. How would I understand what I owed to the various companies that sent me bills? And how would I write a check?

My kitchen drawers and cabinets were nearly as incomprehensible. Some jars and bottles were recognizable shapes, but most of the boxes and cans were indistinguishable. *There's another issue.*

When Mom returned with the groceries, I said, "Tell me what each item is, and I'll put them all away." I lined up the goods on the counter or placed them strategically in the refrigerator. I wasn't ready to try to identify and organize every item that was in my kitchen—just enough for the next several meals.

After I put the groceries away, we all sat in the living room. Again, my parents offered to do whatever they could to get me settled, but like earlier, we couldn't think of anything that needed to be done.

"Are you sure you'll be alright by yourself?" Mom asked.

"I think so. If I have a problem, I'll call you."

"Call if you need anything. You know we're only ten minutes away," Dad said as he closed the front door behind him.

There I was. Alone, and at home. It was just what I thought I wanted, and it was a large leap forward in this journey I'd been thrust into.

I had no future plans. My calendar had no dates to go back to work, get counseling, start rehab, or anything else. I didn't even have a mental list of what *should* be on my calendar. No plans and no knowledge about the challenges before me.

I sat back on the sofa. What should I do? What can I do? Before, I would've taken this down time to read *Sports Illustrated*, mow the lawn, go see friends, or maybe get started on that deck I was going to build. None of this seemed possible now.

I got busy feeling my way around (looking at?) the rooms in my house again. I needed to confirm where things were and what all was there to build a picture in my mind. I needed to feel comfortable and confident in my surroundings.

Living room: Sofa, TV, stereo, and coffee table. As I felt the top of the TV, I knocked over a picture, which knocked into another picture that fell behind the TV. Oops! It was a picture of Chris and Kelly, which made me smile, even though I couldn't see it. On the side table, I "found" a glass of water that Dad had left. Oops again. Now I needed a rag to clean up the spill.

I pictured the geometric print that hung above the fireplace and the other inexpensive print above the fish tank, and when I did, it refreshed my picture of my living room.

Two more bedrooms. Check. I knocked over several toys and knick-knacks in Kelly's and Chris's bedrooms. Why weren't things where I expected them to be?

In the dining room, I came across the telephone answering machine, and pushed the large play button. The machine was filled with three weeks of messages. Many were very touching, but sometimes there were terrified messages from friends.

"Bill, I don't know if you'll ever hear this message, but I wanted to tell you I'm thinking of you. It just doesn't make any sense, and it's not fair."

"Bill, I'm so sorry. You're a great guy and don't deserve this. I hope you hear this message."

The goodbyes were very uncomfortable, so much so that I couldn't listen to all of them. I'd largely escaped the shock, sadness, and helplessness that I heard in their voices, and I felt for them, but I wasn't ready to hear how other people had experienced this yet.

I continued my exploration. Finished basement: check. Workshop: another project to figure out. And how would I make sense of the washer and dryer controls?

I went back upstairs and out to the front porch to sit on the porch swing. It always brought me fond memories. I'd bought it at a woodworking shop in Defiance, Missouri, the day my kids and I had taken our bikes to ride on the Katy Trail, a repurposed railroad right of way that runs across the state of Missouri. Chris was riding his two-wheeler and Kelly was perched in a child seat on the back of my bike. It was such a fun day, and this swing always reminded me of it.

I guess we won't be doing that again, I thought.

I heard cars passing my house. Occasionally one would honk. Was it honking at me? Should I wave? Would I look like an idiot waving if they weren't honking at me? Did my neighbors know what had happened to me? Would they really drive by and honk without stopping? I didn't have any information to help answer these questions and was starting to get a little frustrated.

My world had shrunk to its barest minimum, only those known items I could identify and had then arranged so that I'd be able to put my hands on them when needed. All I had were those few items and the people who would gather with me in person or on the phone. My world felt very small.

But it wasn't like the terror I'd felt in the hospital. It was more like boredom. I couldn't read the newspapers or *Sports Illustrated* or anything else that I enjoyed. I couldn't jump in my van and go wherever I might want to go—to a restaurant, a friend's house, or anywhere. I really had to think about what I could do to occupy my mind and quash the boredom.

The radio! I thought. I went inside to turn on my stereo. I remembered how to find the "on" button and could tune to a station I liked. *This isn't so bad,* I told myself.

Next, I decided to try walking up the street. My block didn't have a sidewalk, so I went down my front stairs and followed the hedge with my hand along the edge of the driveway. When I got to the street, I turned to the left and found the slanted curb along the edge and followed it with my foot. Up the street I went, keeping close to the curb.

Thunk! I'd walked into a parked car. Oh yeah, I'd be looking out for the next one. I followed across the front of the car and down the side with my hand. At the rear, I picked up the curb again and continued on. I found another car bumper and negotiated it successfully. Back up the curb to another bumper. I followed across the front and up the driver's side.

Whack! Something hit me in the face. I felt it with my fingers, and figured out that it was a mirror. The bumper was attached to a truck, and the mirror was big and high enough to smack me in the face. Another bit of information to file away: watch out for truck mirrors.

At the corner, I wanted to cross the street to find where the sidewalk started, but I was afraid that if I left the curb, I might not be able to find it again. The curb was my trail to get back home. But a voice in my head kept trying to convince me that if I walked across the street, perpendicular to the curb I knew, that I would hit the curb on the other side of the street and could just step up onto the sidewalk. I took a tentative first step and paused.

It's only twenty feet, the voice said. *You can do it.*

I could picture the whole intersection in my mind. *What could possibly go wrong?* the voice kept asking.

I decided not to risk it and headed back toward home. There were still vehicles in my path, and I successfully negotiated them all, even the truck mirror. Then I realized that my driveway would be coming up soon.

Was it after the third or the fourth automobile? I couldn't remember. *Had one of the vehicles left? Will I be able to recognize my driveway?*

I'd only thought about going up the street, not about finding my way home again. If I wasn't careful, I'd walk right past my driveway. And then how would I be able to tell it from the next one, and the next one? And then I'd be lost.

I started walking with one foot on the curb and one outside on the grass, so I'd know when I got to the first driveway past the third vehicle. I was relieved to find it, and then there was my hedge a couple of feet into the yard. I was home.

The next day my neighbor, Francie, came over.

"Bill, how are you? I was so shocked when I saw you on TV."

"I guess I'm OK. I just can't see anything. You saw it on TV?"

"Yes, it was big news," Francie said. "They said you were shot in the face, but you don't look like it. The first couple of days really sounded like you would all die, so I'm really happy to see you. What are you going to do now?" she asked.

"I guess I'll try to go back to work," I said. "I haven't really figured out what to do next."

"It's just so unfair that this could happen to you. But you sound good. You might look a little rough, but you sound good. Let me know if I can do anything to help."

Things progressed for days with Mom and Dad wanting to help—but nothing really big to help with—and me feeling bored. Friends invited me out, and I went to dinner with Mom and Dad. Katherine came in almost every weekend, as well. These were welcome diversions, but I felt some urgency to move forward with my life. I couldn't stay in this unproductive, dependent state for long.

Life became more and more frustrating. Cooking, washing clothes, paying bills, needing help—it all added up to a life of dependency. I remembered the settings on my washing machine and dryer, but I needed someone to sort the clothes for me. Mom agreed to take over paying my bills. I didn't have any secrets in my checking account, but what forty-one-year old wants his mother reading his mail and paying the bills?

Pizza and Chinese delivery became the staples of my diet. Getting and keeping track of groceries seemed complicated, and cooking an appealing dinner seemed pretty optimistic. One night I wanted to open a can of pork and beans, but I didn't know which can was which. I grabbed a couple that seemed about the right size and shook each of them, listening for an identifying sound. They sounded a lot the same, so I picked one and opened it. Green beans. *Why do I even have canned green beans?* I thought as they went in the garbage disposal. The next can I opened was pork and beans, and I laughed at my trial-and-error approach.

Another day, I decided to fry some bacon. I'd become accustomed to using my finger to push food onto my fork and spoon, but I was quickly reminded that wasn't a good idea when trying to pick up the cooking bacon with a fork to turn it over. *Ouch!* Lesson learned.

Every bit of every day was new to me, feeling things rather than looking at them. Would I be able to relearn my world and the skills I needed with minimal concessions to the things I couldn't do? I approached every moment with a childlike eagerness to learn. I felt things with my hands and recognized what they were. I approached every obstacle as a puzzle to solve and thought about how I could work around each challenge.

And I also found a lot to laugh about, particularly myself. The pork and beans vs. green beans was only one of many funny situations.

———————

A few days after I came home, the phone rang.

"Hi, is that Bill Johnson?"

"Yes, who's calling?"

"I'm Ray Schaeffer with The State of Missouri Rehabilitation Services for the Blind."

"Well, you've called the right place," I said.

"We think that, with the right help, blind and visually impaired people can have success in their personal and professional lives. Would you like to get together?" he asked.

Of course I did, so we scheduled a time for Ray to come visit me.

I'd already figured out that making notes, keeping and retrieving telephone numbers, and keeping a calendar were things I couldn't do. Dad and I'd brainstormed a solution and decided that I needed a hand held mini-cassette dictation player, and he bought me one. I recorded a note to myself about the day and time that Ray would visit. It went on the same tape with all my other notes, questions for doctors, telephone numbers, and other thoughts. This recorder became my memory. But it had a big limitation. The more notes I made, the longer the recording got, and the harder it was to find anything I wanted to retrieve—another problem for which I had no solution.

The list of things I couldn't do was mounting. I couldn't sort my clothes, go shopping, or read my mail. My diet had narrowed to scrambled eggs and tuna salad, and I was getting to know the pizza delivery guy too well. I knew I couldn't continue this way.

Finally, the day came to meet Ray Schaeffer. That's when I began to learn about a variety of tools that would solve many of the problems I was having, tools that could make the world accessible to me. Ray gave me the names and toll-free numbers of several companies that sold devices that would allow me to do things I couldn't or help me adapt to the things I already owned—clocks, thermometers, bathroom scales, and other things that had audible features. He told me about the National Library Service (NLS), also known as the Talking Book Program that Helen Keller had helped found. Before long, I was signed up with the NLS, and I received one of their tape players. Listening to books and magazines on cassette tape immediately provided me with entertainment and helped curtail my boredom. I even got my beloved *Sports Illustrated*.

Ray also gave me my first bit of mobility training. "I'll show you a technique called sighted guide. You'll find it handy, even after you get a cane. When walking with another person, many blind people find that it's easier to hold *their* right elbow with *your* left hand. You can follow along with the other person that way. They won't even need to tell you when they come to stairs. You'll be a step or so behind them and will feel their elbow go up or down with the stairs before you get there. Just follow the elbow."

"I guess I've been sort of doing that for the last week or two," I said, "but I didn't know it was an actual technique."

"When you're ready," Ray continued, "my primary job is to get people who are blind back to work." Going back to work was on my mind, but I didn't have a plan to do it.

"I want to go back to my previous employer in some capacity, hopefully to my old job. But I don't know how that will work."

"I'll have to talk to your employer. If they're committed to having you return, the state will pay for you to attend a blindness rehabilitation facility in Little Rock, Arkansas, called Lions World School for the Blind. It's supported by the Lions Clubs all over the country."

"What would I learn there?"

He described the range of skills and services they offered: daily living skills, Braille, orientation and mobility (use of a cane), and technology training for talking computers and optical character reading scanners.

"That sounds great. When can I start?" I asked.

"Assuming your employer is supportive, you'll need to make a commitment to stay there for one year. We want to see you successfully returned to work and believe that leaving before completing the full year would be a waste of our money."

"I don't know if my job and clients can wait a year," I said. "Consulting isn't like making widgets. And it's not good for my kids to have their father away for a year. We've all been through a traumatic event, and I need to be a regular part of their lives."

"I understand, and I'm sorry, but that's our offer," he said. "It's a one-year commitment or nothing. I'll talk to your employer, and we can get together again whenever you want."

This news was a shock. I hadn't been thrilled with going out of town at all but had become comfortable that Little Rock was the closest option. But not for a year. How could it take a year to learn to live and work as a blind person?

It had been only six or seven years since I'd lived in Little Rock, and the name Lions World sparked a curious vision. I dredged up a forgotten memory of driving by their facility and seeing quite a few blind people walking around with white canes.

I wasn't happy about the one-year commitment but was intent on getting some training. Katherine, my ever-supportive sister, gave me the names of several other well-known schools for the blind around the country, and I started making calls. The Hadley School in Winnetka, Illinois, seemed like the best fit. I had several conversations with them but wasn't ready to commit. They also suggested a longer residency than I wanted.

Meanwhile, I was increasingly frustrated with my lack of skills and the overriding feeling that I wasn't capable of negotiating most of my life. I had no way to walk around safely outside my home, and I didn't have any way to acquire new information. I couldn't see how going back to work would be possible at all. Further, the time I was able to spend with my children was limited and greatly restricted.

One particularly frustrating day, I called Ray. "Will you come over again? I'd like to talk more about the one-year commitment and explore other options with you." Ray agreed and we made an appointment for a few days later.

CHAPTER
EIGHT

It was good to get out of the house every day, even if it was only to go to the doctor. None of the doctors I'd seen in the hospital had completely eliminated the possibility of my seeing again; several extended the hope that as the swelling went down, there might be some improvement.

I called the Barnes Department of Neurosurgery to schedule my first checkup and asked to speak to Virginia.

"Bill, how are you doing?"

"I'm OK, but I'm getting a little frustrated," I said. "There are a few things that I have trouble doing. Today I need to make an appointment for my checkup."

She gave me a date and said, "I look forward to seeing you."

Dad drove me to the appointment, and it was about this time that I noticed my sensitivity to how other people drove. Dad was a wonderful man and father, but when he was behind the wheel, he seemed to be doing battle with the other cars. Lots of acceleration, hitting the brakes, and muttering about other drivers' intelligence. It seemed contrary to the man he actually was and made me uncomfortable to drive with him.

Virginia greeted us when we arrived, and she sat in as Dr. Dacey examined me. All seemed to be going well.

"I want to see you again in two weeks," he said, "but call us if anything changes."

After he left, I asked Virginia a question that had been hard on my mind. "Is there really a chance that I'll ever see again?"

"That's not a neurosurgery question," she said, "but I know a good neuro ophthalmologist who will give you an honest answer."

"That's what I want," I confirmed.

I made an appointment to see Dr. Custer. On the day of my appointment, I decided to take the trip alone. I wanted to hear this information for myself, by myself.

I'd seen Saint Louis County Cab drivers give my grandmother rides years ago, and since that was the company I'd always used to get to the airport, I called them. But after making the appointment, I started to worry that I wouldn't know when the cab pulled up in my driveway. *Will he leave if I don't come out?* Plus, I couldn't read room numbers or even find the elevator in the medical building. *Will he help me get to the elevator and into the doctor's office?* I sat on my front porch swing, so I could listen for the cab.

When I heard a car pull in, I walked down the stairs to meet it.

"Mr. Johnson?" a voice asked.

"Yes." I said. I felt along the side of the car and found the back door. As I got in, I said "I'm blind, and I'm going to a doctor appointment at Barnes Hospital."

I played him the address from my voice recorder, and we took off. On the way, I asked if he could show me all the way up to the office.

"I'd be happy to," he said.

"When I need to go back home, will that driver come all the way up to the office also?"

"They're supposed to," he said. "Just tell the dispatcher the address and room number."

Maybe this adventure will be successful, and I can use cabs to give me the freedom I need to get around town independently, I thought.

When we arrived, the driver parked and opened my door. He walked around to my side of the cab and asked, "Would you like to take my elbow?"

"Yes." I said. I wondered, *Do all the cab drivers know about the sighted guide technique that Ray taught me?*

He showed me all the way up to the sign-in window.

"Can you please sign me in?" I asked the receptionist. "I can't see anything."

"Sure, just give me your name."

I was then taken back to the examining room. The doctor and I spoke briefly about Virginia. I told him that she trusted his opinion and knew that he'd be honest with me.

"I need to know if there's a chance that I'll ever regain any vision," I said.

"You're sure you want to know?" he asked.

"Yes. I'm not holding my breath for a miracle, but no one seems to be able to shut that door, and I need to know for sure."

Dr. Custer looked into my eyes. "Not good," he said. "Your optic nerves look grey and dead. Functioning optic nerves look alive." He also described the significant retinal damage to both eyes.

He then told me what I came to hear. "There's no way that you'll see again, not with the state of medicine today." Very direct and just what I wanted someone to tell me. Lead with the truth. Follow it with long-shot optimism if you must, but give me the truth first

I thanked him. He was waiting for me to react as though he'd given me bad news, but I said, "I've had some time to get comfortable with this, but I needed someone to tell me the truth. The other doctors were hard to pin down."

A week later, the incision on my head felt very tender and seemed a little moist. I called Virginia.

"Come back in, and we'll take a look at it," she said.

For some reason, I thought it was appropriate to tell her that driving down with my dad felt a little harrowing to me.

"Is there any way you could stop by my house on your way home?" I asked.

"We don't normally do house calls," she said, "but where do you live?"

"Webster Groves. How about you?"

"I'm in Richmond Heights, so that's not too far. Give me directions to your house, and I'll see you around 5:15."

I heard her car pull into the driveway and met her at the door.

"Thanks for coming over. I can't believe I actually suggested it," I said.

"It's OK. I just live down Big Bend, close to Clayton Road. Just don't get used to it," she teased. "Let's see what's going on."

She looked at my incision and diagnosed a slight infection. Antiseptic ointment was all I needed.

It was good to see her again, and I thanked her for this special treatment.

When Ray came back, I explained all the reasons that neither my job nor my family could or should have to wait a year for me to plug back into my old life. Ray explained that they have a lot of experience at Lions World, and their experience told them that one year was necessary for newly blinded people to accept the idea of being blind, to make the decision to go on with their lives, and to learn the necessary skills to be productive and safe.

"Tell me what your workday was like, so we can talk about the skills you'll need," he said.

"I traveled almost every week, out of town to client sites," I said. "There, I interviewed client and vendor staff while taking notes. I also had a lot of client material and technical documentation to read. Then I'd organize what I learned into client reports, which I was often responsible to write and present."

We then talked through the Lions World curriculum. We agreed that I'd already acquired some of the daily living skills that they taught, such as packing a suitcase, taking care of personal hygiene, signing my name, identifying cooking utensils, cooking a meal, and tying a tie. He thought I could probably demonstrate those skills rather than spending a lot of time in class learning them, and that could be the starting point.

The other subjects they taught were more relevant and much needed: orientation and mobility, keyboarding, Braille, and accessible computer technology. We agreed to fill my days with these necessary classes and trust that I could quickly demonstrate proficiency with the daily living skills.

But I still didn't want to stay for a year, and Ray presented an interesting offer.

"Would you agree to stay until you've reached proficiency in these new areas? If you can master them in a month, you can leave, but if it takes a year, you'll have to stay."

I agreed. I knew I needed to learn these things, but I was betting that I could learn what I needed in a few months. I had no intention of taking a year off. By then, my job would have vanished. *And*, I thought, *my kids wouldn't know me.*

I called a friend from my former days in Little Rock when I worked for Southwestern Bell. Jerrell Mullens and

I had worked together and become friends. We'd had a lot of fun and had spent time together in Hot Springs. My fond memories of Arkansas included the horse races at Oaklawn, water skiing at Lake Hamilton in Hot Springs, and eating barbeque.

"Hey Jerrell. It's Billy Ray."

After working together for a few months, Jerrell had announced that I wasn't like most of the Yankees that Southwestern Bell sent to Arkansas. "You might even work out," he'd said. "But you just don't have enough names. We'll call you Billy Ray." And it stuck.

"Well I'll be," he responded. "How in the world are you, Bill? I heard you were trying to get famous."

"Oh, you heard about Atlanta?"

"I sure did," he said. "All kidding aside, how are you doing? You sound good."

"I'm OK. Probably better than the news reports made me out, but I'm definitely blind."

"That's what I heard. It's really a shame. How are you doing with it?"

"That's why I'm calling," I said. "Have you ever heard of a place called Lions World?"

"Of course. I've driven by it my whole life. You and I have even driven by it."

"Well, it looks like I'm going to go there to learn a few tricks. And maybe after that, I'll be able to go back to work."

"They have a very good reputation," he said. "We see blind people walking around in that neighborhood—and even downtown—with an instructor behind them. I guess they're learning to use a cane. Let me know when you're going to be there, and we'll get some barbeque.

It seemed serendipitous that I'd be going to rehab in a city I'd actually seen and where I still had friends.

Aside from navigating the world as a blind man, I had one other major frustration. My bad marriage had turned into a worse separation, which had become a final divorce about six months before I was shot. The divorce was just as contentious as the rest of our relationship had become, and now my blindness and abilities became a point of great disagreement. Kelly and Chris were the leverage.

My ex-wife agreed to let them visit me for a few hours, but not overnight initially. I resisted this idea because I'd just spent two years getting a divorce decree without such restrictions, and I didn't want to tolerate supervised visitation with my own children. I knew I could get my kids fed and cleaned up. And that I could "watch" them safely. We would play with Legos® or something else and stay inside. We—together—would figure out this aspect of our lives.

Laura was adamant in her position, and I was advised that if I wanted to see my kids anytime soon, I should relent. At first, my parents or a friend would come over when Kelly and Chris visited. These initial visits were only for a few hours, a couple of times a week. They were largely uneventful. We invented a game called "Keep the Kids Out of the Kitchen." I would kneel in the doorway to the kitchen, and they would try to get past me by jumping, climbing, running into me, or any other means they could imagine. I loved the physical contact, and we'd all get a big laugh as one or the other broke past me.

I'd ordered a Connect 4 game from one of Ray's catalogs, a vertical tic-tac-toe game that had four columns and rows. The red pieces had a hole drilled in the middle of them, and I could easily distinguish them from the black ones. Kelly and I spent hours playing this and had great fun.

I soon found out that, while adults found it difficult to understand what it's like for a blind person, it was nearly impossible for five- and six-year-old children. One time that became dangerous for me. We lived about a block away from a small park, and before I was shot, we used to walk there to swing on the swings and play on the playground equipment. On windy days, we liked to fly kites in the softball fields. We got pretty good use out of that park.

Kelly, Chris, and I walked there one day, so they could play on the playground just like old times. All went well, and they had a great time. On the way home, I held Kelly's hand as we walked. I knew we would come to a fence to climb over and that the walk to that point was clear. We walked and chatted and then *Bonk*!

"What was that?" I asked.

Kelly had walked me directly into an oak tree. My forehead was scratched, and I was bleeding a little, and poor Kelly was very upset that she'd let me get hurt. She took her responsibilities very seriously. I told her it was no big deal, and we continued walking home.

It didn't take long for me to want Kelly and Chris to spend the night, but my ex-wife insisted that if they were to stay overnight, a sighted adult had to be present. My time with the kids was always on her terms—always. I knew I didn't have a choice, so I agreed to have another adult spend the night with us. For many reasons, we agreed that having an LPN stay overnight was the best solution. The ones who came were all fine people, but this arrangement became very old, very quickly. I thought it sent a bad signal to my kids about their dad's capabilities and was, overall, a bad precedent. I didn't need to bring strangers into my house for my kids to be safe with their father. But I wasn't in control, and that's what we had to do for the first couple of months.

CHAPTER
NINE

During the eight weeks since the shooting and before I went to Little Rock, I'd received several assurances from upper management that I would have a job whenever I was ready. I greatly appreciated all the support, and I was humbled that my life had garnered the attention of men I didn't personally know but knew by reputation.

Jon Madonna, the Chairman of KPMG Peat Marwick at the time, called me at home a couple of weeks after I left the hospital. I'd spoken to him briefly while I was a patient at Emory University Hospital, and we now talked for some time. He seemed genuinely saddened by the events in Atlanta and expressed concern about my future. His words to me were more than reassuring. "Your old job—or any other position you want—will be waiting for you."

"I am hoping to return to my old job," I answered. "I'm not certain how—or if—it will work, but that's what I want to do. I can't even imagine any other role."

"The firm and I will support you in any way we can," he said. "When you're ready, let me know if you have any problems getting the support you need from our side."

"Thank you very much," I said. "It means a lot that you've taken a personal interest in me." This was a man who could back up his commitments, and I felt quite reassured that I'd get a chance to return to the job I knew and loved. All I wanted was to see if I could do it.

The managing partner of the Saint Louis office, Vince Cannella, was also very clear that he was committed to my return to work, although it wasn't obvious what I could do in the Audit and Tax practices that he managed directly, along with the office space. I'd been part of the consulting division and had a different management structure.

Mr. Canella didn't have much insight into my injuries, and the news stories had given the impression that I was in much worse shape than I ever was. He'd called me early on when I was still in Barnes Hospital.

"Don't worry about having a job," he said. "You'll have a job in the Saint Louis office whenever you're ready. I'm not sure what you'll want to do, but don't worry. Even if it's working in the reproduction department, you'll have a job."

"Thanks. That means a lot to me," I said. "I hope to return to my old position, but we'll have to wait and see how it goes."

Only later when I thought about what he had said, I had to chuckle. I didn't know much about being blind yet, but I was pretty sure that I'd be particularly bad at operating a Xerox machine in the reproduction department.

A consulting practice is somewhat like a law firm. Billable hours are everyone's measure. Plus, it was a very entrepreneurial environment. The higher you were in the organization, the more responsibility you had for selling projects and keeping the other staff chargeable. As a senior manager, I was responsible for sales, as well as individual and team chargeability. I didn't want reduced goals or a non-client service position. I wanted the chance to perform my old job on the same terms as I had before.

Our Infrastructure practice had always reported to a large IT practice in Chicago that had responsibility for much of the Midwest. Tony's boss—and the head of this Strategic Services practice—was a man named Roger.

Roger had always been supportive of Tony and our Infrastructure practice, and I was comfortable that he would give me a fair shot. Now that Tony was gone, we reported to Ken, an IT partner in the Strategic Services practice, who reported to Roger. Ken was located in Chicago, and we had never met. His background was large enterprise software systems.

Our Infrastructure practice included three separate practice areas: Telecommunications and Networking, Data Center, and Security. I'd been the head of the Telecom and Networking group, and the leaders of the other two practice areas were located in Chicago and Minneapolis.

Tony's loss to us was massive. He was the glue that kept our three related practices together, as well as our partner interface to the rest of the firm. Tony understood and loved all three of our practice areas. He saw them as footholds in emerging areas of technology that offered significant growth opportunity in the future. He was very forward thinking. The following ten years proved him to be correct, as the term *Infrastructure* came to encompass both the Networking and Data Center technologies and the exploding discipline of IT Security.

Not everyone, however, saw the wisdom of having smaller practice areas, even when they were profitable. Ken was one of them. He was used to sales of $1 million and up; our sales were in the range of $100,000, but they had significant add-on and implementation project expansion opportunity. It was a different practice model than he was used to.

Since he was taking over for Tony, Ken called a meeting in Saint Louis for our whole team. There were about twenty of us at that time. Even though I was a long way off from working again, he called to ask if I would like to attend.

"Yes," I answered, even though more immediate things than work held my attention.

"I want to learn what you all do and discuss how we will go forward," he said.

"Sounds like a good idea," I said.

"Do you have any plans, yet?" Ken asked.

"I'm leaving for rehabilitation in Little Rock in a couple of weeks, but I'm not sure how long I'll be there. The outside is a year, but I can't see how it will take more than several months."

"OK," he said. "I'll see you at the meeting next Friday."

On Friday morning, the doorbell rang. It was Linda, a coworker. We'd worked closely together on consulting projects for the three years I'd been at KPMG Peat Marwick and were both admirers of our late boss, Tony Lake. She'd offered to give me a ride to the meeting.

It was the first time we'd seen each other since the shooting. As usual, Linda was very upbeat.

"What do you want me to do?" she asked.

"Is your car in the driveway?"

"Yes," she answered.

"I'll find the car. When we get downtown, you can let me hold your right elbow when we walk."

"Easy enough," she said.

As she drove downtown, we discussed what we thought the purpose of the meeting might be. We agreed that Ken seemed like a nice enough guy, but none of us knew him well, and he didn't know our practice.

The meeting started like many. We went around the room, and everyone introduced themselves, explaining which part of the practice they were in and what they were working on. We all knew each other, so this exercise was solely for Ken's benefit. The meeting lasted most of the morning, and Ken must have said some encouraging and uplifting things, but what I heard was not encouraging in the least.

"Tony's loss was shocking and terrible, but it's been seven or eight weeks, and the business needs to go on. Bill won't be back for some time. New business booking has gone way down since the events in Atlanta. You all have a golden opportunity to step up to the plate and generate new business. Niche practices like yours have reported to me before in Dallas, and I had to close them for poor performance. I'm not sure that any niche practice is capable of performing like the firm needs it to, so go out and convince me that I'm wrong."

It sounded like he viewed our practice as a problem and expected it to die away from lack of productivity. He didn't offer us any help to sell some big jobs or to lead us to success. He was watching and waiting for us to fail.

In the consulting business, the first thing that must happen—and continue to happen—is for someone to make a sale. It's presumed that the work will be completed on time, on budget, and in a professional manner. That's called delivery. While each consulting project has its own challenges and none are completely straightforward, selling the work is much more creative and much less defined, and it's the start of the cycle.

Tony had been our primary business generator. Also responsible for sales were the lead of the Data Center and Security groups, and me, the Networking and Telecom lead. And I was out of the picture indefinitely.

It was a scary meeting. When it was over, we all went our separate ways. Since most of the group was from Chicago or Minneapolis, they left for the airport before we had a chance to talk.

On the drive home, I asked Linda, "Are you staying busy?"

"I stay as busy as I can. I'm finishing up projects that were still open and talking a lot to the Financial Service practice to see if they have any projects I can help with. I have a couple of possibilities in our field, but nothing real close"

"What did you think of Ken's talk?" I cautiously asked.

"He scared me," she said. "I didn't hear him make a commitment to continuing our practice. What did you think?"

"The same. I don't think we can count on him, but I hope you can stay busy until I come back. I'm not real clear about how all the aspects of my job will work with me being blind, but selfishly, I know my return will be smoother if you and others are still around."

I was concerned that by the time I got back to work, there would be no practice to return to. I'd pictured myself slipping back into my old role with the same team around me. It was much more difficult to picture starting from scratch with no team and no projects, while I was also learning to work as a blind person.

I was convinced that I needed to get back to work as soon as possible, despite the assurances from upper management that I'd have a job. I wasn't so sure. Over the ensuing months, almost everyone in our practice found a spot in other groups or left the firm. Everyone was gone, except for Linda and Bill, both of whom were in Saint Louis. If a mass exodus had been Ken's intent, his message had been received loud and clear. Three years of working with Tony to grow our practice had slipped down the drain.

I didn't see myself being able to save the day, but I did know that if I had any hope of going back to work, it was critical that some part of our team would still be there.

But first, I needed to learn how to function as a blind man.

CHAPTER
TEN

Dad flew with me to Little Rock. I took his elbow, and we successfully negotiated Saint Louis Airport security. It was my first experience with getting special treatment. We were ushered to the front of the line, and I was pleasantly surprised that they seemed comfortable with getting a blind person through security.

"Stand here and reach out both hands," the security person said as she positioned me in front of the metal detector.

Someone grabbed my hands and pulled me through the metal detector without a problem. Next, I had to gather my things from the conveyor belt. I carefully felt my carry-on bag to make sure it was mine. It occurred to me that I must be careful not to pick up the wrong bag. Maybe I should add a unique tag that I could feel.

The flight to Little Rock was rather quick.

"Would you like something to drink?" the flight attendant asked.

"Bloody Mary mix, please," I said as I felt for the tray table release on the seat in front of me. I pulled down my tray table.

The flight attendant opened the can and poured the mix over ice. She set the glass and half-full can on my tray table, picked up my right hand and gently placed it on my glass.

"Got it?" she asked.

"Thanks," I said.

I felt around my tray table for the can. Once I knew where both the glass and can were, I felt comfortable that I wouldn't spill either one. When I finished the first drink, I thought about pouring the rest of the mix into my glass. I could either ask Dad to do it or pour it myself and risk spilling some. Bloody Mary mix was messy.

I grabbed the glass with my left hand, stuck my index finger into the glass, then poured the mix with my right hand until I felt it hit my finger. Success! Another puzzle solved.

When in Little Rock, we took a taxi to Lions World and found the office. The receptionist told my counselor, Marge, that I'd arrived and introduced us. Marge asked us to follow her and her guide dog to her office to discuss my case. She asked many questions about what brought me there at that time.

"How were you blinded?"

"When did this happen?"

"Only two months ago?" she asked. "Who shot you?"

"Are you taking any medications?"

"Do you have any prospects for working when you finish here?"

After that brief meeting, she assured my dad that I was in good hands. We said our goodbyes, shook hands, and he left for the airport. As I got familiar with Lions World, I wondered what Dad must have thought about it. There were about 125 blind students and most of the staff was also blind. While the facility was nice enough, it was an older building, and I doubted that it had been updated in the decorating department. Everything was functional and, of course, there was no one to decorate for.

I stayed in the counselor's office after my dad left. She repeated many of the questions that I'd answered when he was there. And I gave her the same answers. Then she asked a new question.

"Who made you come here?"

"No one," I answered.

"Didn't your father make you come?" she asked.

No. It was all my idea," I said.

Finally, she let it drop.

Later in my stay, I was again questioned about who had forced me to come to Lions World. And I finally found out what created their belief that I was there against my will. Apparently, as Ray Schaeffer had maintained, it really was rare for someone to willingly go to blindness rehabilitation during the first year. It was the staff's experience that the process of grieving the loss—and ultimately accepting the fact of blindness—took at least a year. Most newly blind people needed to stay at home that long before they could get their emotions under control, accept their situation, and decide to make the best of it. I thought back to my hour of acceptance in Barnes Hospital and was grateful it had come so quickly. Now I could concentrate my thoughts and actions on my future without dwelling on the past

Again, this whole one-year time frame was foreign to me. I was driven to learn the skills I needed as quickly as possible. It was the only way for me to regain the life I'd had two months before and continue my relationship with my children and my employer. If I'd stayed at home for a year before starting the year of rehabilitation, I'd have had a different life to build upon. I pictured myself being unemployed with a disability; it wasn't nearly as appealing as going back to my old job.

Marge was the first blind person I'd met in many years, and she was already the one I'd spent the most time with during my entire life. She gave me my schedule of classes and helped me record it on my dictation machine.

"You'll know Braille faster than you can believe," she said. "Then you won't need that recorder anymore."

"We'll see," I said. I wasn't convinced.

Marge showed me to my room, which was another new experience. She held the harness for her guide dog in her left hand and asked me to take her right elbow. We were a wide load, but we made it to my room. Talk about the blind leading the blind!

Along the way, we got onto an elevator. I felt around to make sure I was facing the elevator door. Side wall, rear wall, front wall, doorway. Whoa! I quickly pulled back my hand. The door had almost shut on it. I was the only one who knew what had happened, and it scared me a little. But it also reminded me to stay alert and remember what I knew about the world while I was learning new skills. I should have expected the elevator door to close, rather than being surprised by it.

"This is your bed, close to the door," Marge said as she slapped the bed. "Your dresser is on the right side of the doorway to the bathroom." She slapped the dresser, and I followed the sound and felt my dresser. The room seemed comfortable enough.

She took me to the TV lounge outside my room, which was shared by everyone who had rooms on that wing of the building.

"The only rule in the TV room is no blankets allowed."

"OK." Seemed like kind of a random rule.

She showed me the route to the stairs that led to the cafeteria and to my first class the next morning. I walked around with my hands out in front of me, like Frankenstein. It was the only way for me to find the walls and corners that were my landmarks.

Finally, Marge left me alone. I put my things away and lay down on my bed. If coming home from the hospital was the first stage of my journey, being in rehabilitation school was the second. It was the next step on the path to learn the skills I needed to be the most productive, comfortable blind man I could be. I was anxious to get going. The next thing on my schedule was dinner, followed by my first class in Orientation and Mobility tomorrow morning.

———■———

"Hello! You must be Mr. Johnson," I heard a voice say.

"Yes. Who is that?"

"Magid," he said. "I'm your roommate."

"Nice to meet you," I said as I got up.

"I heard you got shot," Magid said. "That's very bad."

"Yes," I said. "Right through the temples."

"How did that happen?" he asked.

"It was a random shooting on the street in Atlanta."

"Was anyone else shot?"

"My boss and our client were killed," I said. This aspect of the story was always difficult to share.

"Oh, my. That's very bad." The anguish in his voice reminded me how shocking the story was to others. Over the past two months, I'd told and retold it so often that it had started to sound like someone else's life rather than my own.

"Yes," I said. "Even worse, my boss and friend, Tony, had five-year-old triplets and his wife was pregnant with another child. Keith, our client, also had a wife and family. I'm certainly the lucky one."

Magid had an old-world formality, and although I asked him to call me Bill, he always addressed me as Mr. Johnson.

"How did you become blind?" I asked.

"I have macular degeneration, and I'm slowly losing my vision. I'm here to get trained to work for the IRS."

"The IRS?" I asked.

"Yes. They hire many high partials to work in their call centers."

"What's a high partial?" I asked.

"People who have partial vision. For example, I'm legally blind, but I can still drive a car when I wear glasses."

"I have a question for you, Magid. Why don't they allow blankets in the TV room?"

"Simple, Mr. Johnson," he answered. "They're concerned that young men and women will watch TV together and have a little hanky-panky under the blanket. There are sighted staff who make the rounds, but they don't announce themselves when they come by."

I was suddenly aware that there was a total lack of privacy in this place. I didn't plan on misbehaving, so I didn't really have anything to worry about, but I had the feeling of being watched all the time.

Magid was a very interesting person and a good roommate for me. A Persian, his family had been wealthy, and his father had been well connected in the Shah of Iran's government. Magid had come to this country to train with our Navy, and eventually, he was to return to Iran as a Navy officer. He was in New York when the Shah was overthrown.

"My family was out of luck. We lost everything, and I was stranded in the United States."

"How long have you been in the US?" I asked.

"About ten years."

He lived in his wife's hometown in Tennessee, and it had been difficult for Magid to stay employed. He thought that *most* of this related to his being Persian, and *some* was related to his failing eyesight. He harbored some strong resentments but was a great roommate for me.

"Do you have a car here?"

"No," he said, "But when my wife visits, I drive when we go to dinner."

What was going on here? I thought this was a school for the blind. Later, I learned that only a small percentage of the people at Lions World were totally blind—about 15 to 20 percent.

One day some of the other residents asked if I wanted to play basketball.

"How does that work?" I asked.

It worked exactly like the basketball I used to play because this group was all high partials. Even in the school for the blind, I was more blind than most of the group, and this news was a little shocking. I'd expected to be part of the community, but now I felt like I stood out as the blindest of the blind.

Rather than get discouraged or depressed, I vowed to keep a positive attitude and simply do the next thing that was presented to me. If I kept moving forward, things would work out. There was nothing to gain from getting angry or feeling depressed. I had to step up.

When dinnertime came, Magid offered to show me to the cafeteria. It was back the way I had come with Marge and up a flight of stairs. We went through a cafeteria line.

"Here's a tray and a plate," Magid said, as I put my tray on the counter. "Follow me."

"Do you want a hamburger or roast beef?" a voice on the other side of the counter asked.

"What else do you have?" I asked.

"That's it for main course. We have some vegetables and desserts further down."

"I'll have a hamburger."

"Reach out your plate, and I'll put it on there."

We got a beverage and sat down to eat. The room was very noisy, all hard surfaces and lots of people talking.

When we were finished, Magid said, "Now pickup your tray. We need to take them over to another counter and pass them through to the dishwasher."

The window was piled with dishes already. Finding a place for mine wasn't easy. I feared that I would accidently knock over a stack. On the second or third day, that's exactly what happened. Magid and I stacked our dishes, and as were walking away, I heard a crash behind us.

"Was that my fault?" I asked.

"Yes," he replied.

The food wasn't great, and the whole process of eating in the cafeteria was always uncomfortable for me.

My first class on my first full day was called Orientation and Mobility. I left my room and followed the route I had traveled a few times, except before I had a sighted guide with me. When I got to the main hall where the classrooms were, I was assaulted with the sounds of chaos. Lots of the "tap, tap" sounds of white canes, and lots of movement as people passed me by. I thought the room I wanted was on the left side of the hallway. I walked a few steps, but I bumped into people or got brushed by a cane on my legs. After a few more steps I said, "Excuse me."

"Yes?" came a reply.

"I'm looking for the O&M office. Do you know where it is?"

"About twenty feet away. Take my arm," the man said. He deposited me in front of a door and said, "This is it."

He banged his cane on the door frame, so I could hear its location. I thanked him and he left.

Standing in the open doorway, I could hear a couple of people in conversation to the left, but they didn't seem to notice me. Then one of them said, "Can I help you?"

"Yes. I'm Bill Johnson, and this is my first day here."

"You'll find a chair about two steps to your left. Have a seat and we'll be with you in a minute."

Soon a young woman, Lisa McDermott, introduced herself to me. "I'm going to be your instructor," she said. "Do you have a cane?"

"No, I'm pretty new to being blind," I answered. "I don't have a cane."

"Come over to my desk. I'll take some information, and then we'll get you a cane."

I stood up and Lisa's right elbow brushed my left arm. I took it, and we walked over to her desk.

"There's a chair in front of you," she said as she slowed down. I found the chair and we sat.

We talked about what had happened to me and I answered all her curiosity questions about the shooter and how long I'd been blind. Then she asked me what I wanted to learn at Lions World.

"I want to be able to get around by myself," I said. "I've been limited to my house or going out with others for eight weeks now, and it's driving me crazy. I don't like being so dependent on others."

Lisa assured me that my goal was achievable if I worked for it, but she didn't know how long it would take for me to get there.

"How do you decide if I've learned enough to get out of here?" I asked, explaining that I wanted to learn quickly and get home to my children.

"That's hard to answer. Orientation and mobility are two different, but related, skills," she explained. "Orientation means maintaining awareness of where you are and where you're going and knowing how to plot a route from here to there. Mobility refers to the cane skills you need to follow the route safely. Do you understand the difference?"

"Yes, I think I do."

"I can teach you the cane skills pretty quickly, but you'll have to practice them a lot to be safe. We don't yet know how well oriented you are, but I'll be giving you some tips. You haven't been blind long, so we'll just have to see how it goes.

"In the final test, we drop you off in downtown Little Rock and see if you can get back to this office by yourself. You'll get lots of instruction before you try it, so don't worry. We haven't lost a student in years," she joked.

"Wow," was all I could say. I couldn't imagine navigating any downtown by myself.

Lisa took me over to a closet. "How tall are you?"

"Five nine," I answered.

She handed me a cane and said, "Put the handle under your armpit with the tip on the floor, and let me look at you." I did, and she said, "That's a little short, try this one."

She liked that one better and said, "Fifty-two inches is the right length for you. Remember that. Do you want a folding cane or a straight cane?"

"I'm not sure," I answered. "How would I know?"

"It's really a personal preference, but some think the straight cane is better for walking a long distance. The folding cane can be stored out of the way when you aren't walking. We can give you one of each, but let's start with the straight cane."

I felt the cane in my hand. It was light. There was a rubber grip at one end with a big elastic loop coming out of that end. One side of the grip was flat. I noticed there was a plastic tip on the opposite end.

"What's this rubber grip?"

"We use golf putter grips. It even has an imprint of a golfer on it," Lisa said.

"What's the elastic cord for?"

"You use that to hang it up. The folding cane will have an elastic loop that's divided, and it has a small loop at the tip of the elastic. You'll use that to wrap around the cane when it's folded up, so it stays folded."

I liked the feel of the cane in my hand. It seemed purposeful, and it made me feel like I was finally ready to start learning. It felt like a tool—like it belonged in my hand. Over the ensuing months I would get very comfortable with my cane.

Lisa explained the theory of using the cane. I'd never paid any attention to any blind person walking by themselves, but I assumed they randomly waved their white cane around to keep from falling in an open manhole. Now I found out there was a specific technique involved.

Lisa explained, "As you walk, whenever your left foot goes forward, the cane moves to the right. When your right foot moves forward, the cane moves to the left. When done properly, you're always clearing the space you are walking into with either the cane or your leading foot. Let's practice this in the hallway."

I took her elbow and carried my new cane out to the hallway. The hall was empty, and I practiced walking up and back, moving my cane back and forth in front of me as Lisa had instructed. When the cane bounced off the wall on my right side, I found that I could use it to locate my path in relation to the wall. Not too close, and not too far to the left if there were people approaching from the other direction. Cool.

As I turned back toward Lisa, she said, "Now work on holding the cane centered in front of you and low. Concentrate on tapping lightly on the left and right end of your range of motion." I'd been holding my hand down by my right side and kind of swiping the cane tip from side to side, so I switched my technique.

"Holding the cane in the center will protect both sides of your body from a collision, and picking up the cane as it moves from side to side will keep it from getting jammed on sidewalk cracks too often. Touching down lightly on each side is sufficient to guard against holes or open man holes." Who would have thought there was this much technique in using a white cane?

I tap tapped my way down the hallway and back several more times, practicing this refined technique. It seemed very natural to me. Step left, step right, back and forth, tap, tap. Hold your hand in front.

"Good. I think you're ready to go outside. What do you think?"

"Let's go."

I took her elbow and followed her to the front door.

On the way, Lisa asked, "We'll be gone for two hours. Do you want to get a candy bar to take for a snack?"

"Sure," I said.

She stopped and started reading off the types of candy bars in the machine. "I'll take a Payday."

"Give me your money," she said. I heard her operate the machine, and I bent over to pick up my candy.

"No, no, no!" Lisa said.

"What?"

"You almost smacked your face into the machine when you bent over. Don't ever bend over that way."

"How should I bend over?" I asked.

"Always hold your hand out in front of your face when you bend over. If there's anything in the way, your hand will hit it, not your face."

Later, the several times I didn't follow her advice, I was reminded of this lesson. I was still moving my body around like I could see what was in the space around me. I never realized how forcefully and purposefully I'd moved when I was certain the path was clear. On several occasions, I whacked my head hard enough to bleed. It was like biting my tongue and being amazed that I bit down that hard on normal food.

Lisa had plenty of tips for me, and I realized how much I had to learn. Beyond being safe, I wanted my blindness to be as inconspicuous as possible. That meant I'd have to learn how to avoid doing stupid things like banging my head on the candy machine.

We stepped outside to a wonderful, warm, late-summer Arkansas day.

Lisa explained, "You're on a concrete walkway that runs from the front door to the sidewalk at the street. There are steps on the sidewalk between here and the street. I want you to walk out to the street and turn right on the other sidewalk. You'll have to be careful to use your cane to feel where the walkway steps down."

"OK," I said. I started off pretty slowly and deliberately, terrified of the steps. "Here it is," I said when I found the first one and stepped down.

Tap, tap, tap. I continued on until I found the next one and the next. This wasn't so scary, and it seemed pretty easy to gauge the location of the next step down. This cane thing seemed to be working. It was certainly better than feeling in front of me with my toe to find the path.

I walked until my cane hit dirt and found that I could stop walking before I stepped onto the dirt. *That must be the street side of the other sidewalk,* I thought. I turned right and took a couple of steps forward.

"Good," said Lisa. "Stop here for a minute. Lions World takes up a whole city block. There are sidewalks on all four sides. You are facing South on Tyler Street, with the street on your left, and Lions World on your right. Does that all make sense?"

"Yes," I answered.

"I want you to walk all the way around the block until you get back here. Which way will you turn at the next intersection?"

"Right. But how will I know when to turn?"

"When you get close to the street, listen for the car traffic. That should help you gauge about where to find the sidewalk to your right. I'll be right behind you, so don't worry about the street. OK, let's go," she said.

I tap tapped my way down the sidewalk. "Ouch!" I said as I came to an abrupt halt. My cane had caught in a sidewalk crack. Holding the cane centered low in front of me created the potential for some painful stops.

"Tap lightly on the left and right, and make sure you pick up your cane in between," Lisa said. "You'll get more comfortable with the cracks as you practice and get better. You were looking good, otherwise"

Tap, tap, tap, tap I went. I could hear the cars passing in front of me. As I neared the street, I slowed. Tap, tap. Just as my cane fell over the edge of the curb, Lisa's sure hand grabbed my shoulder.

"Did you feel the curb?" she asked.

"Just as you grabbed me."

"I just wanted to make sure. Since you found the street, where's the sidewalk you are looking for?"

"It must be behind me and to the right."

"Find it for me."

I turned ninety degrees to the right and felt with my cane. Dirt. The sidewalk must be off to my right a couple of feet, I thought. I turned to my right again, and felt to my left as I took a couple of steps. I tapped the ground with my cane. Dirt, Dirt, concrete.

"There it is," I said. I turned left and continued toward the next intersection.

This is working pretty well, I thought as I made my way down the block. I was able to feel the grass on the left and right with my cane to assure myself that I was on the sidewalk. Suddenly, the grass on both sides ended. Within a couple of steps, I stopped. I tapped all around me, turning around and looking for the grass. No grass. I was lost.

"Where am I?"

Lisa said, "This is a driveway that you have to cross. It's where the garbage truck picks up our trash. Go back to the sidewalk, turn around, and try it again."

"I don't know which way to go."

"Here's something else you'll learn: what did you do when you realized you were off the sidewalk?"

"I turned all around to feel for the grass."

"Yes, you did. And you lost your orientation when you did that. What you should have done was stop, turn 180 degrees, and take a couple of steps back to the grass edged sidewalk. Then you could turn back around from a known location and listen for clues to understand the situation that confused you. Never start spinning around aimlessly. You'll always end up disoriented." Lisa offered me her elbow and showed me back to the sidewalk.

"Now, I told you this is a driveway, so you need to walk straight across it to find where the sidewalk continues. You might want to back track several steps just to get a good straight line of travel across the driveway."

I did as she suggested. The driveway seemed to be as wide as a football field. The farther I walked, the more tentative and lost I felt. Finally, my cane struck dirt. I stopped and considered what had gone wrong. *The sidewalk must be to the left or right several feet*, I concluded. I felt several feet to the right. No sidewalk. Back several feet to the left. There it is. Back in business, I headed to the next corner and another right turn.

At the next corner, Lisa asked me to stop.

"Come over here and feel this," she said as she slapped something.

"What is it? Feels like a sculpture. Is it an animal?"

"It's a lion," she said. You can use it as a landmark when you walk around the building if you get confused about which corner you're on."

I reached out to feel what she was describing. "Wow, it's really big. Mouth, a big mane, and here's the tail," I said. "I'll try to remember where it is."

We made it around all four corners without Lisa having to grab me again or me impaling myself on my cane. Success. The side to side tap, tap, tap reminded me of an old-fashioned metronome. The weighted rod going back and forth was like my cane sweeping back and forth with a steady rhythm. Tap, tap, tap. Just like the metronome tock, tock, tock.

As we turned the last corner, Lisa said, "Now I want you to find the walkway to the building."

"How do I do that?" I asked.

"Which side will it be on?" she asked to question my orientation.

"On the right."

"Correct. As you tap your cane on the right side, make sure you touch the grass. When you get to the place where there's no grass, you've found the walkway."

This whole O&M thing really resonated with me. It was all very logical. As long as I could maintain my orientation, I could think through what to do. This first trip with my new cane was exhilarating. It felt very natural, and it worked! Finding my way around felt like a game. How could I get from here to there using logic and cane technique? I enjoyed the challenge, and Lisa was a great instructor.

I followed her instructions and found the walkway to the building. This time I felt the "up" stairs with my cane and negotiated them smoothly. I reached the front door and was very proud of myself.

"Good job," Lisa said. "Do you have any questions?"

"No, but that was fun."

"Good," she said. "Let's do it again before lunch."

On my fourth trip around the block, Lisa stayed behind—or at least she said she had. How would I know? She told me to make the trip by myself, find the sidewalk to the front door, and turn on it.

Down the first side of the block. Tap, tap, tap. Stopping before the street, I found the next side of the block and off I went.

Driveway, stay straight, I said to myself as I slowed my pace. Oops, grass. I tried left, and heard myself getting closer to the street. Try right. There's my sidewalk! Tap, tap, tap. Next corner, turn right. I continued around the block.

As I found the walk to the front door, I heard "Good job, Bill. What's that big grin about?"

"This is really fun, and I can see how it works," I said.

"Good. How did the walk go by yourself?"

"The only problem was that big driveway. I don't know how I'll learn to walk straight for thirty feet. I veered left this time, but I thought it through, listened for the traffic in the street, and I found the sidewalk."

"Good job. If you pay attention to all the cues around you and stop to think when you get confused," she said, "you'll be fine.

"It's almost lunchtime. Use your cane to walk up these steps to the front door. Make sure to find each step and judge where to step up. We'll work more on going up and down stairs tomorrow.

CHAPTER
ELEVEN

That afternoon and into the next day, I was introduced to the rest of my classes: Keyboarding, Braille, Math, and a group of Daily Living Skills. I threw myself into all of them. Mastering each was my ticket back to Saint Louis. But I was also truly intrigued and challenged by learning new things and learning how to do old things in new ways.

Before I'd come to Lions World, Ray Schaeffer had told me that personal computers could be outfitted to speak the words that appeared on the screen. We agreed that one of these computers would be essential for me to get back to work. But before I could get a talking computer, I'd have to demonstrate proficiency on the keyboard.

I'd taken typing in ninth grade, but my memories were not fond ones. In high school and college, I'd typed my own papers, but that had been twenty years ago. And even though this was 1991, I'd proudly resisted the PC revolution of the late eighties. While some of my more forward-looking coworkers wrote client reports on a PC, then sent them to the Word Processing Department to format and print, I still handwrote everything on legal pads and gave them to Word Processing or to my administrative assistant to type. Then I made corrections and edited the work by pencil, only to wait for the next version to come back to me. That method wouldn't work anymore. Time for me to enter the twentieth century!

After my successful morning of learning to walk with a cane, I headed down the hallway past the O&M office after lunch. I knew the typing room was further up on the left. When I got closer, I could hear the distinctive clack of typewriters. *Great, that must be the room.*

From the doorway, I asked "Is this the typing class?"

"Yes sir, what's your name?" a female voice responded.

"I'm Bill Johnson."

"I'm Mrs. Miller, Bill. I was expecting you. Follow my voice and I'll show you to your desk."

I ran my hand over the top of the typewriter. It felt like an IBM Selectric, the kind with the printing ball. I tried to remember how the letters were arranged on the keyboard.

"Did you ever learn how to type?"Mrs. Miller asked.

"A long time ago I could type enough to get by. But I wasn't all that good. And I could see back then."

"Let's see how you do," she said. "First, let's insert a piece of paper and set the margins."

I'd been so concerned about remembering which keys were in what spot that I forgot about the paper. She showed me a trick to make sure that the paper was straight as it rolled into the typewriter, then showed me how to set the margins.

In the ninth grade I'd learned touch typing. That meant that rather than looking at my hands as I typed, I was supposed to keep my eyes on the paper I was typing. Didn't everyone fudge that as much as they could? Did anyone but a secretary really learn to type without looking at the keys? I'd disregarded that direction as much as I could, but now touch typing was back in my world with a vengeance.

Mrs. Miller gave me a small tape player and headphones. The audio contained several paragraphs, no doubt designed to make me use all the keys that I couldn't remember. Like the quick brown fox and other classic typing ditties.

"There's a story for you to type on this tape. Turn in your paper to me at the end of the period."

Amazingly, the letters and shift key came back to me pretty easily. Z and X were a little hard to remember, as was Q, but I felt pretty good about how my memory served me. The numbers and punctuation were another story.

I turned on the tape player and typed away. Over the ensuing days, I practiced a lot. Sometimes I was timed, and the results were inspected for errors. I had to achieve forty words per minute with no errors. My first scores were twenty-something words per minute, so I kept practicing.

Load the paper, make sure it's straight, set the margins, type type type.

One day, I had a longer piece to type, and I tore into it. Type type type, Ding, hit return, type type type. After some time, Mrs. Miller tapped me on the shoulder.

"What are you typing?" she asked.

I told her, and she said, "Hand me your paper."

I reached for it, but there was no paper in my machine.

"I know I put the paper in," I said. "I wonder what happened?"

"Look on the floor," she said.

That seemed ridiculous. How could I "look" on the floor—or anywhere else? Then I understood. I'd typed and hit return so often that I'd typed right off the bottom of the page, and the paper had been ejected. I cracked up. The thought of me typing on the roller and loading it up with ink was hilarious. Nothing to turn in for much of my hour's work, but still, I got a good laugh.

During the third week, I'd reached the forty-words-per-minute-with-no-errors hurdle, and I was reassigned to the technology lab and a talking computer.

———▬———

For the first several weeks, I was also scheduled for classes in various daily living skills. These classes, along with the Keyboarding and Braille classes, were in rooms on either side of a long hall. At the end of each class, a bell would ring and all the students would emerge from the rooms, turn left or right, and proceed to their next class. No problem, right? But everyone was blind and most had white canes. A few had guide dogs. It was chaos with much bumping and jostling and an occasional cane slapping the floor as it was kicked out of someone's hand.

On one phone call back to my doctor's office, Virginia asked me what the school was like. I described this be-tween-class routine to her.

"Everyone's going from one random room to another with no rhyme or reason. I think there's probably a little groping that goes on. You know it's a co-ed school," I joked.

I eventually learned that there was a system to the mad-ness. Keep to the right of the hall. *Wait a minute*, I thought. *These people are blind. They've never driven cars. How do they know to keep to the right?*

After I'd conquered my first daily living skill—actually getting into the classroom—I was ready to immerse myself in Daily Living Skills. I made it my mission to test out of these skills as quickly as possible, so I could move on. For example, polishing shoes.

"I get that done at the airport," I told the instructor. Apparently, I thought I was much funnier than she did. She humored me while I polished a pair of shoes. Who knows if I did a good job or how much polish I got on my hands? I figured she couldn't tell either. I easily passed this test, but my plan was to stick to the guys at the airport.

Signing my name? I passed that on the first day, but it made me think about how many of their twenty-something students might not know how to sign their name. I was truly grateful that I hadn't been born blind. I had a head start on the rest of my life, having been sighted for forty-one years and during those important, formative learning years.

Packing a suitcase? This was one I should ace. I'd been packing and traveling in my career for twenty years. When I failed suitcase packing several times, I thought I'd better learn how to do it the way the teacher thought a suitcase should be packed. Her method would have been fine if my suitcase could travel lying down, but I didn't think it would fare too well when it stood upright. All heavy items will shift to the bottom. But I did it her way to pass the test and decided I could continue packing the way I wanted to.

Grooming: Really? Apparently, my baseline was higher than some of the other students. Along with knowing how to pack a suitcase, Lions World provided me with a constant reminder of how grateful I was for the life I'd had, and the life I could have, if I worked for it.

Identifying cooking utensils was next. The teacher handed me each utensil one at a time.

"What is it, and how would you use it?" she asked.

"Spatula, to flip a hamburger; ladle, to get soup from the pot to a bowl; cheese slicer, to slice cheese." On and on it went. "Carving fork, to hold the meat as you carve it with a knife."

These skills were all pretty simple. Fortunately, I'd had a lifetime of experience to draw from. These were the very classes I'd convinced Ray Schaeffer that I didn't need. Demonstrating my mastery quickly would confirm what I'd told Ray and propel me forward, so I could get home for Thanksgiving.

In the meantime, I was getting better with my cane. It wasn't exactly the same as walking down the street as a sighted person, but with a cane, I could walk independently and arrive at my destination—just like when I was sighted. The fact that the walk required more of my attention and was a near-constant exercise in logic and problem solving made it more fun. The occasional pratfalls and the need to re-orient myself and get back on track were part of the fun.

Finding the right storefront, sticking my head in and asking, "Is this the gift shop?" was the proof of my new ability. If the answer was "Yes," I felt successful. Sometimes the answer was, "No. This is the dry cleaners. You need to go one more door." Even though I'd been mistaken, now I knew where the dry cleaner was, and I added its location to the map I was building in my head. I'd also made another friend.

The Braille class was a different story. I knew this would be a helpful new skill and was intrigued to finally figure out what those indecipherable markings on elevators were all about. We'd all heard of and seen Braille, but who had ever taken the time to figure out how to read that strange alphabet?

My instructor said that each Braille character was made up of a subset of six dots, which was called a *Braille cell*. The cell contains six possible dots arranged in two columns of three dots each. Each letter of the English alphabet is a subset of the possible dots. A is the upper left dot. B is the upper two on the left side. C is the two top dots. Dots also indicate punctuation and capitalization. In the simplest Braille, Grade 1, there are symbols for prepositions, and each letter standing alone means a specific common word that starts with that letter. Grade 2 Braille is more akin to shorthand, where common portions of words, like "-tion" and "-ing" have simple Braille interpretations.

With that as my orientation, the teacher gave me a textbook to use to learn the symbols.

The book had raised representations of English alphabet letters, with the Braille equivalent next to it. A through Z. I studied this until I knew it. Some letters were intuitive—like L was the three left side dots, shaped like a lower case "l."

The A through J signs are all represented in the top four dots. The K through T signs are the same as A through J but with an additional dot in the lower left of the cell.

It was fascinating to feel the raised letters on the page. I use my right index finger, tracing the capital A. It felt about an inch tall. Then I felt the Braille dot for A next to it. The raised English letters in the book were easy to identify. The Braille letters were harder to distinguish. Toward the end of the study book, the Braille letters became much smaller. While this allowed a single letter to fit under the tip of my finger, it made the individual dots much harder to differentiate. This smaller version was the standard size of Braille. The larger format in the front of the book was for teaching each letter and training the finger and brain to this new function.

I also got a slate and stylus for writing Braille. The slate consisted of two pieces of steel, about the size of rulers, that were hinged together on the left side. The top ruler had several horizontal lines of rectangular cutouts, each the size of a Braille cell. Each cutout had enough shape to suggest where the six dots of the cell would be located. The bottom ruler had corresponding indentations below each of the cutouts. To position this to write, I lifted the top ruler, slid a piece of paper under it and against the hinge, and closed the top piece over the paper.

The stylus was a small, blunt punch, about the size of a stubby screwdriver. By using the slate as a guide and pressing the paper with the stylus, the indentations on the lower ruler served to receive the stylus and allow it to press the Braille dot into the paper. Using this device, I could write Braille by hand. But Braille dots are raised, and this method indents the dots in the paper. How would that work?

"You write from right to left," the teacher explained, "and form the mirror image of each letter. That way, when you turn the paper over, you can read from left to right with the dots raised."

Was this going to be my life? Carrying around this prehistoric-seeming slate and stylus and writing notes backwards with it? It was very slow, and I wasn't perfectly accurate. What role would this play in my life? I thought that I shouldn't worry about how the many things I was learning all fit together and how they'd each help me shape the productive, happy life I envisioned. I figured the more skills and options I had, the better I'd be able to do what I needed to do in the real world.

In Braille class, we were also trained on a Braille typewriter. I thought it probably looked like an antique. It had a steel frame like an old portable typewriter, but there were only nine keys that stuck out the front. It seemed like this was a typewriter that hadn't changed since the turn of the nineteenth century. At the top was an opening where I could insert paper, and there were two moveable stops for setting the margins. When I inserted the paper, it rolled completely inside the machine, and as I typed, the paper emerged as I hit the carriage return, one line at a time. Very different!

I used the typewriter in class to transcribe simple sentences and demonstrate my knowledge of the alphabet for when I wanted to write. But reading Braille was a different animal.

When I demonstrated that I'd memorized the alphabet, I progressed to reading simple things like the *Dick and Jane* books. No kidding. This was exactly like learning to read again.

First, I had to recognize each letter individually, but by the time I'd felt the last letter in a word, I'd forgotten the first one, so I had to backtrack. It was slow and tedious. Then I could move on to the next word, but by then I'd forgotten the previous word. It was frustrating, but I kept after it.

I liked the fact that I could lie on my bed with the book on my stomach. No need to look at the page I was reading. Bonus! No eye strain from reading either. Added bonus! I tried to recognize the letters more quickly, which made remembering the previous letters, recognizing words, and remembering the previous word easier. After a couple of weeks of practice, I read "See Dick run." Straight through. No backtracking for forgotten letters or words.

This might work, I said to myself! It tickled my memory about how much fun reading used to be, and it brought a smile to my face, even though it was a child's reader. I'd made progress on another one of the skills I needed to master.

——————

During my first week at Lions World, I met with the staff psychologist.

"This first meeting is part of your onboarding here," he explained. "We can meet whenever you want and will certainly meet at least one more time shortly before you're released. The purpose of today's meeting is to get to know you and learn if there's anything troubling you that you want to share."

"OK," I said.

"It says here that you were blinded in a shooting on July 2. Was that this year?"

"Yes."

"Just two months ago?" he asked.

"Right."

"That's what this information says, but I assumed it must be wrong. That's very quick for you to be in rehabilitation. How have you reacted to being blinded?" he asked.

"I guess pretty well, but I need to learn some new skills and new ways of doing other things."

"What have you been doing since July 2?" he asked.

"I spent three weeks in the hospital between Saint Louis and Atlanta. When I was released, I went home," I said.

"That was just five or six weeks ago, right?"

"More like eight weeks," I said.

"How did those weeks at home go?"

"OK, I guess. I was frustrated with some things, and I was bored a lot."

"Did that make you sad about the fact that you couldn't see anything?" he asked.

"Not really sad. More frustrated, but only at times."

"Are you angry about being blind?"

"No," I said. "Maybe angry that my friend, Tony, was killed, but not at my being blind."

"Are you angry with the man who shot you?"

"I don't really feel anger toward him," I said. "Just angry that my friend was killed. I didn't see the man who shot us, so it's hard for me to identify his actions as the cause."

"Do you feel guilty in any way for you all getting shot?" he asked.

"Not at all," I said. "This was completely random."

"Do you feel any guilt for surviving when your associates didn't?"

I hadn't considered that before. "I don't think so. I haven't really thought about them a lot. I know what happened to them, but I guess I've been a little focused on myself."

We continued on for the remainder of our one-hour session, and my answers created my baseline evaluation.

———

It was finally time for me to visit the technology lab and to begin the talking computer class. The classroom was upstairs in a separate building that I hadn't yet visited, so I asked a few people on the way for directions. I eventually found it.

"First, let me show you all of the adaptive devices we have here. This is a Kurzweil Reader. Come over here and feel it," Angela, my instructor, said.

"It's big," I said.

"Yes. It's essentially a copy machine, but rather than making copies, it reads printed text from pages that are put on the glass top. There's already a document on the glass, so I'll push the *read* button, and we'll see what happens."

With that, a very human-sounding voice started speaking the words that were on the paper.

"There are nine different voices. If you don't like this one, you can pick another one."

"That's neat," I said. "Do many people own these?"

"Not too many," she said. "They're pretty expensive, but they're often available in various blind service organization offices. Also, PC-based versions are becoming available using a scanner. The controls are a little more confusing, but they work fine, and they're a lot less expensive."

We moved on to the other technologies in the lab.

"Here, take this cane," Angela said. "It has a laser or a radar or something in it, so the handle vibrates at a different rate when you come to an opening, like a door. You don't tap it like your regular cane. You just move it back and forth in front of you and feel the various vibrations in your hand."

"Can I try it?" I asked. The vibrations were pretty subtle, and I asked, "What's the point of this?"

"I'm not totally sure," Angela said. "It's just something that's available if you want to use it."

Then we made it over to a computer. "Did you ever work with a PC when you were sighted?" she asked.

"Very little," I said. "I bought a Windows desktop last winter, but we mainly use it for games with my kids."

"This computer has a DOS operating system and Word-Perfect, a program for writing documents. The computer is made accessible to the blind by installing a specialized program that produces an audible feedback with every key stroke. It allows you to create, read, and save documents on the computer. DOS computers are very accessible. The Windows operating system is not as accessible yet."

"That sounds good." I said

"Sit here, and I'll walk you through how it works," she said as she slapped the back of the chair. "Now find the keyboard on the table in front of you."

"Got it," I said as I started feeling around on the keyboard to get oriented. The little dots on the F and J keys were never so valuable.

She showed me the process of booting up. When the computer came on, it said aloud, "Dec Talk," the name of the adaptive program.

"Now enter wp and hit enter, to launch Word Perfect," Angela said.

"W P Enter," the computer said as I typed. Then, "WP51," announcing that Word Perfect version 5.1 was open.

"It always opens up to a blank document," Angela said. "Your cursor is in the top left corner of the page. Can you find the up and down arrow keys? We put raised dots on them and on the left and right keys."

"Are these them?" I asked.

"Yes. Now hit the down arrow, and see what it says."

I found the down arrow and pressed it.

"Blank," the computer said. I hit it again and again.

"Blank, blank "

"The program always opens up to a blank document," Angela instructed. "And the document doesn't have a name. Go ahead and type a few lines of anything."

"T H E space Q U I C K space B R O W N . . ." The computer began speaking as I typed that old paragraph that made me use all the keys.

"Now, go to the up arrow and hit enter," she said.

"The quick brown fox jumped . . ." the computer spoke as it read the first line of the document.

"That's a pretty mechanical sounding voice," I said.

"Yes, but you'll get used to it. Most people think it's more understandable when it's speeded up, even more understandable than the more human-sounding voice on the Kurzweil Reader."

Over the next few classes, Angela taught and I practiced. I created and named documents, found the one I wanted in the directory, and deleted documents. We worked on searching for words and a few other simple tricks that made the program easy to use.

One day, Angela told me that they had a new program that could make a Windows computer accessible. We fiddled around with it for a bit, but it didn't seem as functional as the DOS computer I'd been using. Email and the internet were just emerging, and I'd had no experience with either.

The good old DOS machine would be perfect for me. I was already planning to type all the notes and phone numbers from my little dictation recorder into a Word Perfect document, which I could organize and search to find information.

CHAPTER
TWELVE

I felt like I'd established a pretty good routine over the first few weeks at Lions World. I attended all the classes and felt like I was learning valuable skills. Magid, my roommate, and I got along well, and we ate most of our meals together. On the weekends, I flew back to Saint Louis to see Chris and Kelly. Going home every weekend was a unique arrangement that Ray and I had negotiated before I went to Arkansas. In fact, I was the only student doing this.

I wanted to see Chris and Kelly as much as possible. They made me happy, and I believed that it was in their best interest to see me every week. They were young children and shouldn't have had their father disappear from their lives, particularly after a terrible accident had rendered me blind. Most of these weekends I got to see them for at least a day, sometimes two. I was convinced that these visits were the best way for them to learn that all would be well. I wanted them to see me functioning in all aspects of my life. They deserved to have a father they could depend on, rather than having me being dependent on them.

My ex-wife's position about me taking care of our children as a blind person had hardened. My visitation periods were defined by her, rather than our divorce decree. She maintained that her restrictive approach was recommended by the child psychologist she consulted, and I accept that she was doing what she thought was in the best interest of our children. I disagreed.

Nevertheless, the uncertainty of everything related to my children was quite upsetting. I was powerless in so many ways. I couldn't drive, and I couldn't get Laura to revert back to a consistent, fair visitation schedule. One of my two major motivators was being the best father I could be, along with getting back to work. I knew that if I lacked any daily living skills, she would use that against me to minimize my contact with the kids. This was a big, immediate motivator, as I feared that not progressing through Lions World, and ultimately back to work, would be held against me in creating a normal life with my kids.

During the rest of my weeks, Magid and I spent a lot of our unassigned time in our room together. We were both fifteen or twenty years older than most of the other students and hadn't gotten close to any of them. Instead, we talked about Iran under the Shah's regime and the revolution, what happened to me, his family and mine.

"I'm going back to my old job when I get out of here," I said. We'd had this conversation several times as we got to know each other better.

One day Magid said, "You don't really think you'll get your job back, do you?"

"Of course I do. Why wouldn't I?"

"Oh, Mr. Johnson. You are so naïve. People do not like blind people. They will never give you your job back. Employers are scared of blind people at work. They think they can't do anything, that they just create problems. Blind people don't fit in with the other workers, and we cost them money. They can't even get rid of us because of the government."

"You're wrong," I said. "I think our country is better than that, and many people in my company have told me that my job is waiting for me."

"They're lying to you, Mr. Johnson. They don't want you to come back, and when the time comes, they will tell you there is no job. Blind people are poor performers at work, and companies don't want them. You'll see, Mr. Johnson."

"Well, I'm going to do everything I can to get ready to go back. I can't control what others will do, but I have faith that most people want to do the right thing, and they'll help people who help themselves. Rather than showing people what I can't do, I'm going to impress them with all that I can do as a blind person—and how well I do it."

"You'll learn, Mr. Johnson," he said, unconvinced.

I could have lost confidence in the future or gotten depressed about my prospects, but instead, I became even more committed to learn what I needed to learn, return to the same job and relationships with my kids that I'd had before, and to do it all well.

But it felt like an uphill battle. My ex-wife, my supposed new boss at KPMG, and now my roommate had all said that they expected me to fail. Further, the world of blind rehabilitation thought I should take an entire year off to learn what I needed to learn and to accept my blindness. I would have none of it.

My mission was to return to my life—that meant a full return to my kids and my work life, but all I heard was their negative messages. Were they right and I was wrong? I didn't know, but I was more determined than ever to return to my old life. I didn't yet understand the particulars of how that would happen, but so far I'd done what needed to be done and had accomplished whatever was in front of me. I just needed to keep learning and stay upbeat and positive. The rest would take care of itself.

———

A few weeks into my stay at Lions World, I got word that the IT leader at the bank I'd been working with in Atlanta wanted me to phone him. When I did, he expressed his sorrow about the events on July 2 for me personally, and for Tony and Keith.

"Thank you for your thoughts," I said.

"We'd like for you to come to Atlanta to present the final report to our leadership team," he said.

"Really? Me, specifically?" I asked. I wondered if going back to Atlanta would be upsetting, but I didn't say anything. After all, his boss had been killed that day.

"Yes," came his assurance.

"I'll have to finish the report before I can present it."

"Whatever you can put together will be fine," he said.

Wow. I hadn't thought much about the details of work or clients since July. How could I get this done? Tony and I were the only two working on this project, and he obviously couldn't help. I couldn't review my written notes or our files to pull together a final report. Plus, I was in rehab in Arkansas and didn't really have time for this.

And how did I feel about returning to Atlanta? Should I feel scared? Uncomfortable? Anything? Nothing? The thought of returning to Atlanta seemed strange, but not scary. I'd have to see how I felt about it as the day got closer.

Right away, I called Linda. Linda had driven me to the meeting a few weeks ago, and we'd worked on several similar projects together, although not this one. I told her what I'd been asked to do.

"Can you find the client file and any of Tony's notes?" I asked.

For once, I was glad that accounting firms had strict requirements for keeping all client notes on an ongoing basis, and that Tony was a big proponent of that. In addition, I assumed my notes were still in the briefcase that had, somehow, made it back with me.

"Would you mind reviewing whatever you can find and meet me at my house Friday afternoon?" I already had a trip home scheduled. "I'm hoping that with those notes and your experience with similar engagements, we can pull together a presentation. The client understands the situation, so we don't need to write a report, just present the key findings and recommendations."

"Agreed. I'll be there Friday."

On Friday afternoon, Linda arrived at my house with the information she'd been able to locate. She read it aloud to me, and we talked through what she'd found. I explained what I remembered about my notes, but I wasn't sure I'd included everything. I'd become somewhat comfortable with my Mom or Dad reading my mail to me, but it felt kind of selfish and needy to ask someone from work to read my own notes to me, but what choice did I have? Of course, it didn't bother Linda at all, and being familiar with the material, she found the important points in the notes and skipped the background information that didn't matter.

We talked through the outline for the presentation, and some preliminary findings and recommendations that had been noted in either Tony's or my notes, and Linda added a few from her review.

That was the easy part. I was very uneasy about my ability to assimilate the information I needed to write this report, and I didn't want to impose on Linda to read and re-read the material to me enough times for me to remember it. I was frustrated that I couldn't take notes or organize my thoughts on paper. I questioned whether I could actually return to my old job. So much information to sort through and analyze.

My normal method of writing a report had been to first review all my lengthy notes and background data. I would read through all the information, start a new bunch of notes that contained only the important facts and start a new page where I put any tentative findings. I'd boil down a large volume of information into a manageable number of pages and identify the information to be included as an appendix. Then I could organize it all into the normal sections of our reports: Work Performed, Findings, and Recommendations.

Could I go through this process without being able to see my notes or, in the future, without being able to take notes? *Those talking computers better be really good*, I thought. But my immediate task was to help write a presentation for this client that would provide them value and give us something to present to them in just three short weeks. Fortunately, consulting work was usually done by a team, and collaboration on presentations and final reports was normal.

Linda, of course, had mastered the information she'd uncovered, and she had experience with similar studies at other banks. She was up to speed.

"Would you mind taking notes as we talk this through?" I asked her the next Friday afternoon. "I know you aren't a secretary, but I don't know any other way to do this."

"Let's go," she said.

Working from the rough outline we'd already put together, we added some substance. Linda had identified good examples from the files, and she added some details to support the broader statements. In short order, we'd completed a first draft. And before long, we'd pulled together a presentation that hit on the major things we'd learned. It was a presentation that I was comfortable making.

As we worked together, I asked, "Do you think this will work?"

"What do you mean?" she asked.

"Collaborating and talking through the solution, with you needing to get our thoughts on paper. Do you think we can get our jobs done like this?"

"We'll work it all out," she answered.

I sure hoped so. I knew that, at this point, I couldn't have pulled this presentation together by myself.

We decided to talk again when this new version was typed up. The meeting was the following Thursday. I would fly from Little Rock to Atlanta, and Linda agreed to meet me in the Atlanta Airport, so we could go to the client together. It was such a relief to talk with someone who supported my coming back to work, rather than those who thought getting back my old job was a pipe dream.

The day finally came for the presentation. I still didn't have any strong resistance about going back to Atlanta, just a sense that it was surreal. That didn't seem like a compelling reason not to go. I was certainly going to face this situation at some point. Why not now?

Since the client knew me, I thought I should do most of the presentation, but I was really nervous about whether I could remember it all. Like most presenters, I'd always used my PowerPoint slides to prompt me with the talking points, but now I couldn't do that. I couldn't even take notes or put up the slides. Linda and I strategized how we might pull this off together, and she read through the slides several times to refresh my memory.

"I think I can remember the order," I said. "Can you advance the slides to keep up with me?"

"Of course," she said.

"Please jump in whenever you see an opportunity, and I'll try to direct any pertinent points to you."

Our contact arrived in the lobby and escorted us to the conference room. Linda wasn't used to me walking at her right elbow. It was new for her and she did well, but I did bump into a table in the hallway on our way to the conference room. I heard a vase or something else on the table wobble, but it didn't fall.

"I'm sorry, Bill," Linda said.

"No problem," I said. No damage had been done. "It's my responsibility, not yours, to use my cane to clear the way for myself. If I bump into things it's my fault."

As we set up in the conference room, the group quickly gathered. Several of them that I'd met before said hello and expressed their condolences for Tony and Keith and for what had happened to me. Our host introduced Linda and me, and we began the presentation.

It wasn't as good as I would have liked, but not as bad as I feared. I was glad when it was over and asked if there were any questions. Rather than fielding questions, most of the comments were to thank and congratulate me for coming in person to deliver the final report. I realized that this group had suffered a blow themselves. Their leader, Keith, had been killed, and their organization still felt his loss. To this day, I believe that completing this project and having me present the findings was more about closure for them than it was about the report.

It also served as a big encouragement to me.

CHAPTER
THIRTEEN

I thoroughly enjoyed travelling home most weekends because it felt like my old life was still intact. I saw family, neighbors, and friends, and I explored my neighborhood while furthering my white cane skills. Now that I could navigate the world with a cane, I didn't ever want to be without one. Every time I went home, I brought another one with me from the O&M office. I'd fold one cane in my bag, and take a straight cane on the plane. Then I'd leave one or the other in Saint Louis. They only cost $16, so I thought I couldn't have too many of them.

I got to be pretty independent when I traveled home, which I thought was good training for my future business travel. One of the Lions World staff members always drove me to the airport, and they'd drop me off at the curb. I'd get a skycap to either escort me to the gate or he'd call another airport employee to do so. This person would direct me through security and introduce me to the gate agent. It was clear that I was blind, so the agent would seat me in the pre-boarding area. Pre-boarding meant there was always room for my bag in the overhead bin.

This system worked well, and I got to meet many interesting people. I always tipped the airport personnel who helped me from the curb to the gate, and from the gate to the taxicab once I'd reached my destination.

After my second trip home, I got back to Little Rock after 8:00 p.m. that Sunday night. I was met by a skycap, and I took his elbow as we walked out to get a taxi for my ride back to Lions World.

"Are you a football fan?" I asked.

"Yes sir," he answered. "The Razorbacks were looking good yesterday."

"Do you think they can beat Texas?" I asked.

"It'll be tough."

When we got to the taxi, I reached in my pocket for some singles to tip him. I had a stack of folded-over $1 bills and another stack of folded-over $20 bills in that pocket. I felt uneasy, but realized I had to trust this man. I grabbed one stack of bills and asked, "Are these singles?"

"Yes sir," he answered. I gave him four of the bills and got in the taxi.

Later, I asked my roommate, "Can you help me figure out how much money I have?"

"Sure," Magid said. He separated out the singles, twenties, and other random bills and counted $88. I knew how much money I'd had when I'd left Saint Louis and how much I'd spent on the trip home. I was around $80 short.

"The skycap took four $20 bills instead of four $1 bills," I said.

"Mr. Johnson," Magid said, "you need to take better care of your money."

Shortly thereafter, I took a class about managing money. But it wasn't about managing money, as in paying bills or retirement planning. This was managing money, as in how to know which bill was what denomination. The system they taught assumed that I'd carry a traditional folding wallet that had an envelope or pocket for bills.

"Fold the $5 bills in half before putting them in your wallet. $10 bills should be folded in half lengthwise, and $20 bills should be folded both ways, so they're only one quarter of their full size. Put these and $1 bills—which are left unfolded—in the bill section of your wallet. Now when you pay for something, you'll always be able to identify each bill in your wallet. When you receive change, ask the cashier to identify each bill, fold it appropriately, and place it into your wallet immediately. Got it?" the instructor asked.

"I think so," I said, "but I carry a money clip, not a wallet."

"Here's a wallet and an assortment of bills you can practice with," she answered. "You'll want to buy a wallet and start using it instead of your money clip."

I wasn't so sure about buying a wallet but agreed to practice this method with the sample wallet to demonstrate my proficiency. I folded about ten bills in the suggested way and put them all in the wallet. It made a lumpy, fat blob—which is exactly why I carried a money clip. I didn't want a big lump in my pocket. Nevertheless, I'd demonstrated that I knew this strategy, and I now had at least one method of keeping money straight when I traveled.

But I couldn't picture myself standing at the grocery checkout, meticulously identifying and unfolding bills, then continuing to stand there while the cashier identified each bill I got in change and folding it just so. If the people in line behind me had car horns, they'd be blasting them at me to get moving.

I never gave up my money clip. Instead, I devised my own method of keeping my money organized. I put $20 bills in the money clip in my right front pocket. One-dollar bills went in my left front pocket. Anything else stayed loose in my right front pocket. This way, I could always safely tip and pay for purchases with twenties and singles. I figured that no one could trick me out of more than $10 with my method, and if they wanted to do that to me, they—like the skycap at the airport—needed the money more than I did. I don't think anyone else has ever tried to take advantage of me with that kind of deception.

Eventually I learned that in regard to many things in my life—including money—I'd have to form a trusting relationship with others because there were many things I'd never be able to do by myself. Like getting my own cash from the ATM. I had a couple of trusted cab drivers who helped me with that. I gave them my card, and to get any money out I had to share my PIN with them. I told them how much cash I needed and they came back with that and returned the card to me. Did I like doing this? Of course not. But in order to be independent, I had to rely on the courtesy of others, and that meant I needed to trust them.

———————

After my trip to Atlanta, it was back to my studies. One of my classes was Math. I'd completed college calculus, so I figured I could master this quickly. I soon learned that the class could have been called Calculator because it was basically about learning to use a hand-held calculator that was modified to speak with every button pressed. In one ear, I'd listen to an audio tape that oriented me to the calculator. There was a different earphone for my other ear that was attached to the calculator.

It didn't take long to get comfortable with the button layout, and after that, it was easy to add, subtract, multiply, and divide. An audio tape instructed me to perform simple mathematical word problems, which I solved using the calculator. Many of them were so simple that I could do them in my head, so that's what I did. I gave the answer without using the calculator. The teacher didn't think that was funny, and she told me I'd have to demonstrate the ability to solve math problems using the calculator.

During the second class, I asked if I could take the proficiency test.

"Don't you need to practice more?" she asked.

"No," I answered. "I'd like to finish up this class."

She was reluctant to give me the test, but relented. "You need 95 percent to pass. You have to get nineteen out of twenty correct."

I took the test and was certain of every one of my answers. *100 percent,* I thought as I handed in my paper.

"Come back tomorrow to check your score," she said.

The next day she said I'd gotten an 80 percent and would have to practice for another day before I could take the test again.

"There must be some mistake," I protested.

"No, you got 80 percent"

"Can you check it again? I know I got 100 percent," I said.

"I don't have your paper with me," she said. "Please sit down and practice today, then you can take the test again next time."

I did as she asked, and on the next try I got 100 percent. Apparently, I needed to humor the teachers. After all, they controlled how quickly I could complete each class. Whether or not I actually passed the first test, I was again aware that I was fortunate to be able to do math, either in my head or using the calculator, and was able to get another skill I needed checked off the list quickly.

The next weekend, I was home on Friday afternoon and called the doctor's office about my medications. I spoke to Virginia. It was good to talk to her again, and this time, we were both in the same city.

After she answered my questions, I thought it would be nice to see her.

"What are you doing for dinner tonight?" I asked.

"What? I guess I don't have any plans," she said, caught off-guard.

"If you drive, I'll buy you dinner. How about it?"

We'd gotten to know each other pretty well over the past couple of months. We shared many laughs and also had some serious conversations. I always looked forward to talking with her, and Virginia seemed like my friend at the doctor's office, not my nurse.

"OK. It's a deal," she said. "When should I pick you up?"

We had a very enjoyable dinner at Gianni's Italian Restaurant and shared much about ourselves over our pasta and wine. I learned that she was single and had a daughter studying Theater and Political Science at Washington University. In addition to her job at Barnes Hospital, she was a flight nurse in the Air Force Reserve at Scott Air Force Base in Illinois. It was shortly after the first Gulf War. She told me that she'd been activated but only made it as far as an airbase outside of Washington D.C. when that brief war ended. I was impressed.

No mention of a boyfriend.

Back home, I invited her in for another glass of wine, and we listened to some music. As she was leaving, I surprised her with a kiss. That's not as easy as it sounds when you can't see your target. But it went well.

"I didn't know this was a date, Mr. Johnson," she said with mock formality.

"I didn't either, but I guess it is," I answered lamely. "Would you like to have dinner again when I'm home next weekend?"

"Sure. I'd like that," she said.

After that, we went out every weekend. I really looked forward to those dates. Our relationship was going well, and it was exciting.

But I had other classes to pass before I could go home permanently. First, I had to learn to cook a meal, and I could choose to cook whatever I wanted. I would make the grocery list, the staff would do the shopping, and then I had to demonstrate that I could cook it successfully. That meal would be my lunch that day.

"I'd like to make some pasta," I said, thinking of a linguini dish I liked to make.

"I'll get you some spaghetti, a jar of spaghetti sauce, and what else?" the instructor asked.

"I wasn't going to make a spaghetti sauce. Could you get some linguini, an onion, a bell pepper, olive oil, butter, garlic, and parmesan cheese?"

"We don't usually get that involved. Is there something else you could make?"

"I guess I could make tacos," I answered.

"That sounds better. I'll get some ground beef, taco seasoning, and shells," she said.

"I'd like two packs of taco seasoning and also some lettuce and tomatoes." I always liked to double up the seasoning for extra flavor in the tacos.

During the next class, my groceries were at hand, and I started preparing my Mexican lunch. I browned the ground beef, drained it, then added water and one-and-one-half packets of the seasoning mix. I shredded some lettuce and diced up the tomatoes. When I tasted the meat, I burned my fingers a bit. It didn't seem spicy enough, so I added more of the seasoning.

The teacher told me that it smelled very spicy, very hot. I didn't smell a thing. Finally, I turned down the heat and made myself two tacos. The meat was somewhat over-cooked, but I ate both the tacos.

"Just the way I like them," I said, figuring that eating the food meant I'd passed the final test for this class. "Would you like one?"

"They smell a little too spicy for me," she said, but she gave me a passing grade.

That afternoon, several other students asked if I'd cooked lunch that day.

"Yes," I answered.

"I could smell the taco meat burning down that whole hallway," one of the men said.

"I didn't smell anything," I said, and it was true. I was just happy to finish up another class. I could refine my cooking skills later.

On another visit home, an old friend suggested that I wasn't able to smell. She put an open bottle of vinegar under my nose without saying a word.

"You can't smell that, can you?" she asked.

"Smell what?"

"I just held a bottle of vinegar under your nose, and you didn't even notice."

"What?" I said. "Let me have it." I reached out my hand and took a big whiff from the open bottle. Nothing.

"Wow. You're right. I can't smell it at all."

I reported this to my doctors, and they said that along with the damage done to my optic nerves, my olfactory nerve had also been severed. Those nerves were close to each other, and both had been affected. Maybe those tacos really were a little too spicey.

"I can't afford to lose too many more senses," I joked. "Pretty soon I'll have no sense at all."

On another visit home, my sister Katherine mentioned that Rich, our KPMG contact from the hospital in Atlanta, had been in Chicago. Together, she and Rich had coordinated a lot of expense reimbursement for her and Dad's trip to Atlanta.

"We went out to dinner a couple of times," she said, "and I guess you could say that we're dating now."

I paused to take that in. "So, I'm in the hospital, maybe won't live, and you're looking for a date?" I teased.

"It wasn't like that," she answered. "He was in Chicago for business in September, and we got together."

"Just kidding," I answered. "He seemed like a nice guy. I hope you have fun."

CHAPTER
FOURTEEN

Within the first six weeks, I'd satisfied the teachers with many of my daily living skills, so my counselor and I met to realign my schedule to include the classes I still needed. We both agreed that I could never get too much Braille. I could always read and write faster, and the Grade 2 version was a real challenge. We agreed that continued practice on the talking computer in the computer lab was also productive.

"We can schedule you for half of an afternoon every day with each of those, but we need to fill up your mornings," she said.

"How about Orientation and Mobility all morning, every day?" I said. I really couldn't get enough of it.

"Do you really want to devote that much time to it? We can figure out other things to fill up your schedule."

"I would prefer to do a half day of O&M, unless there are other classes I don't know about. O&M, technology, and Braille are the three skills that I'll use daily. I'd like to improve them."

"That's fine with me," she said. "I'll type up a Braille class schedule for you."

She'd been right the first time I met her. No more micro-cassette recorder for my class schedule or anything else. I could now read Braille—at least enough to follow a class schedule.

My mobility instructor, Lisa, and I spent every morning together, and I was thrilled. We'd already spent a lot of time walking around a neighborhood that had sidewalks and not much traffic. Some of the sidewalks didn't have a strip of grass between the sidewalk and the street, but most of them did. That grass buffer was like having a marker on both sides of the lane on a highway. I had learned to walk pretty straight and could straighten myself out in response to gentle contact with the grass on either side. If I didn't overcorrect and change my angle too drastically, I could walk at a pretty good pace.

But without the grass strip on the street side, I felt I needed to hug the grass or a building on the side away from the street. I was also reminded that light poles, street signs, and parking meters were close to the street. Staying away from the confusion they offered was important. I needed more practice.

"When you step on a sidewalk crack, try to make sure you're crossing it at a right angle. As you practice, use that information to stay straight as you walk down the sidewalk—without having to touch the building or the grass.

"OK," I answered. "I haven't been paying attention to that. I'll have to start."

My major challenge in these neighborhoods was to figure out where the street corners were, so I wouldn't walk down a wheelchair ramp and into the street without knowing it. If there was no sound of traffic to alert me to an approaching street, I had to pay close attention to how far I'd walked and try to feel with my cane for any variation in the pavement that would indicate I was on a ramp or in the street. If there was no cross traffic, missing an intersection and crossing a street wasn't dangerous. But it would cause me to lose my orientation. Once I'd lost my orientation, I'd have to figure out where I went wrong and where I was now, which was really difficult. Even figuring out what direction I was facing was a challenge.

If Lisa had said, "Go two blocks, but don't cross the street. Then turn left for four blocks and cross the last street. Then turn right for two blocks and cross the street," I could get lost at any street that I'd crossed unwittingly. I wouldn't even know I was lost until I heard traffic on the wrong side of me, or found that a sidewalk had ended, or some other such unexpected situation. It would be almost impossible to backtrack to solve the riddle.

So, wheelchair ramps were a particular frustration. I'd never given them much thought before, but now I longed for a distinct high curb at every corner. Then I wouldn't miss an intersection. It crossed my mind that city planners must not know how difficult these curb cuts were for me, and I thought, *How often do you see wheelchairs on the street?* A very selfish thought that I only entertained briefly. Of course, I hadn't even thought of baby strollers.

The more I practiced, the easier it was to identify each intersection, regardless of the cross traffic. I started to feel like white canes and wheelchairs could coexist on the same sidewalks. Soon, I made these daily walks with Lisa a game. I tried to walk as fast as I could without impaling myself on my cane at a sidewalk crack and without missing an intersection. My stride lengthened as I became more comfortable. Tap, tap, tap, my metronome signaled as I walked down my well-defined lane.

———◼———

Ray Schaeffer visited Lions World about eight weeks into my stay. I was one of several students he was there to check on.

One morning, he joined Lisa and me on our neighborhood walk. Here was my chance to show Ray how quickly I was progressing.

"OK, Bill, let's see how you're doing," Ray said.

I took off with Ray and Lisa behind me. I'd become pretty familiar with the route I was walking, and I knew there were only a few spots where I sometimes got confused. I walked as fast as I safely could. Straight down the sidewalk, feeling those cracks to minimize the need for correction. Right up to the street corner. Listen for traffic. Cross the street. Turn left. Listen for traffic again. Cross this street and proceed. Long strides. I was really moving. I only had a couple of minor missteps, and was able to logic my way through them without Lisa's help.

When we finished, Ray said, "It looks like you're doing well with your cane."

"I love it," I said. "I wish I'd had one in Saint Louis when I got out of the hospital."

"You're also making good progress on the rest of your courses," Ray said.

I was elated. "Thank you, Ray." Getting his positive feedback felt great. We walked back to the cars at a more leisurely pace and went back to Lions World for lunch.

———■———

During these months in Arkansas, it was fun to see my old friend, Jerrell from my Southwestern Bell days. We renewed our friendship and re-visited some old haunts, like McClard's Bar-B-Q in Hot Springs and Simm's Bar-B-Q in Little Rock. At Sims, Jerrell and I reminisced about the day we'd had lunch with Bill Clinton.

Sims is an old-time barbeque stand. You order at a counter and find a seat at one of several large round tables. The tables seat six or eight, and you often end up sitting with people you don't know as the restaurant fills up. One day, Jerrell and I sat at an empty table. Just as we started on our baby back ribs, the currently ex- and future governor of Arkansas, Bill Clinton (he served two non-consecutive terms), entered the front door with a friend.

It always amazed me that Jerrell could create an instant rapport with everyone. And he seemed to know almost everyone who lived in Arkansas.

"Hey Gov, come sit with us," Jerrell hollered as he slapped the top of our table.

"I'll do that, but I need to get some ribs first," Clinton replied. They brought their trays over and Bill Clinton sat in the chair to my right. "How are you fellas doing today?" he asked.

"If I was any better, I couldn't stand it," Jerrell said. Then he extended his hand to the other man. "Hi, Jim Guy," he said.

"Hello, guys," Jim Guy said.

That name rang a bell. *It must be Jim Guy Tucker*, I thought. He would be Bill Clinton's Attorney General when he was re-elected and would succeed him as Governor of Arkansas. He ultimately got caught on several improprieties and spent some time in prison.

Bill Clinton was absolutely charming. He asked where we worked and about our families, but he didn't really share anything about himself. Definitely a gifted politician.

Another time, Jerrell came to Lions World wearing his clown outfit. He enjoyed volunteering with the Shriners. He wore a full clown costume and visited hospitals and other places where kids who need some cheering up might be found. This Sunday afternoon he was still wearing his clown costume when he came to pick me up.

"Those people out there were sure staring at me," he said.

"Why was that?" I asked.

"Feel my shoes," he said.

"They're huge."

"Yeah, I've been clowning this morning," he said.

"Who's outside?" I asked.

Someone else interjected and said, "They're entertaining some donors and Lions Club members on the front lawn."

"They have a tent set up, and everyone's all dressed up," Jerrell added. "Are you ready to go?"

We walked out, and I took Jerrell's elbow.

Jerrell said, "If I thought they were looking at me before, they're staring at us now. They're thinking, 'There goes a clown with a blind guy. Is that OK?'"

That image cracked me up.

We got in the car and took off for the restaurant. As we pulled into the parking lot, Jerrell said, "Johnson, would you look at the hooters on that one?" as he slapped me on the chest. "Oh, I'm sorry," he said reassuringly. "You can't see that can you?"

My friends. It was good that we could laugh at my changed circumstances. Many situations I got into were really funny, and I was grateful that I could laugh at my own antics. Like leaving the blind school on the arm of a clown.

CHAPTER FIFTEEN

"Today we're going to downtown Little Rock and will learn about traffic signals and busy streets and sidewalks," Lisa said. "Are you ready?"

When I'd lived in Arkansas before, I'd walked these same sidewalks, but not often enough to remember the location of many of the businesses. I remembered the big office buildings and a few other things, as well as the general look of downtown Little Rock. The thought of more crowded sidewalks, busy streets, and traffic lights was intimidating. *How will this work?* I asked myself.

"I'll be right behind you, so don't worry about a thing. Just use the skills you learned in the neighborhood, and you'll be OK." Lisa said. "Now walk up to the next corner. Just stand there and listen to the traffic. See if you can hear when the traffic signal changes from red to green."

Where we were standing, a loud city bus took off and a horn honked. More going on here than in the quiet neighborhood. I pictured eighteen wheelers cutting sharp corners and hauling their trailers across the corner of the sidewalk—where I was standing—and other downtown traffic disasters. A little scary!

I gritted my teeth and said, "I can do this." *Tap, tap, tap.* Off I went.

"The sidewalk doesn't have a grass strip on either side," Lisa warned.

I decided to stay close to the building. That felt safer than being on the street side. I reached the intersection and stopped. As I listened to the cars stopping and starting, I began to picture what the traffic signals were doing.

"Green light next to us," I said to Lisa as I heard the cars to my left take off.

"Right," Lisa said. "Listen for when they stomp on the gas pedal and the engines roars. That's your cue that the light turned green. You should start crossing the street in front of you when they first start up. That way you'll be walking with the green light and should get across before the light changes."

Cross the street. I remembered many of these downtown streets being four lanes wide, plus the parking lanes.

"How can I keep walking a straight line across that distance?" I asked.

"Listen for the parallel traffic and keep the same distance away from it all the way across," Lisa said. "Let's give it a try at the next green light."

I heard the roar of the cars to my left as they accelerated and took off parallel to them. *Tap, tap, tap, tap, tap, tap, tap.* Would this street never end? Had I missed the curb? Was I walking down the parallel street? What would happen when the light changed if I was still in the intersection? My mind raced. I gritted my teeth and kept moving forward. *Tap, tap, tap, tap.*

Bump. I finally found the curb and was never so happy. As I stepped up onto the curb, the cars behind me surged away. The light had just turned green for them, and I'd made it across safely.

"Nicely done!" Lisa said. "You are about ten feet away from the corner. It's normal to shy away from the parallel traffic a bit, but you'll want to work on walking straight across the street. Turn right here, and let's walk a few blocks.

Turn left at the next intersection. Walk to the next cross street and stop. Listen for the signal, and then cross that street."

"OK," I said and took off.

We spent many hours in downtown Little Rock, and I became more comfortable with listening for the light changes. It was harder to figure out the left-turn arrows and to anticipate traffic turning in front of me on a green light.

Lisa reminded me, "The turning traffic is not going very fast, and it isn't normally a problem. They see you and will stop, or you'll hear them and stop."

That proved to be true. One time I was crossing a street, and *bump*! there was a car in my path, engine running. I was confused. What was a car doing here?

"I veered too far from the parallel traffic?" I asked Lisa.

"Yes. What should you do now?"

"Follow around to the front of the car and continue on to the curb?" I asked.

"Yes, and don't waste any time. The light is getting ready to change."

This happened less frequently as I got better at keeping myself lined up with the parallel traffic.

One day, I discovered a new challenge. As I was walking down a sidewalk, I hit the side of a parked car. The engine wasn't running. *No curb between me and the car, so it isn't parked in the street,* I thought. I couldn't imagine why a car would be parked on the sidewalk. I turned around a couple of times to try to figure out the puzzle, then walked around the car one time.

"I give up," I said to Lisa. "What happened to my sidewalk?"

"Did you step off of the curb?" she asked. "Where could you be when a car is parked, but not in the street?"

"Hmmmmm" I said, as I thought. "A parking lot?" I asked.

"Yes," Lisa said. "Now find your sidewalk."

Oh, no. I just walked around in a circle and became disoriented, I thought. I moved slowly around in the parking lot, finding other parked cars. I couldn't make any sense of their direction or grab onto any clue to get reoriented. I couldn't figure out where I'd left the sidewalk. Lisa let me struggle for fifteen minutes without a comment.

"I'm lost," I finally said.

"What was your first mistake?" she asked.

"Veering off the sidewalk?" I asked.

"No. You forgot to freeze when you first realized that something didn't make sense. When you first bumped into that car, you should have frozen right there and thought about the situation, rather than walking around the car and spinning around. Do you remember the driveway at the back of Lions World?"

"Oh yeah. I should have stopped when I first hit the car."

"That's right. Have you been paying attention to the sun's location while you walk?"

"No. Why should I do that? And how?"

"Let's walk over here in the sun. Can you feel the difference when you're in the shade versus the sun?" Lisa asked.

"Oh yeah. I can when I think about it."

"Now turn around until you feel the sun hitting you directly in the face."

I did as she requested and stopped when the sun felt the warmest on my face.

"Perfect," she said. "Whenever you're walking, make a note of where the sun is in relation to your path—left, right, forward, or behind you. When you get really disoriented, the sun can help you reorient yourself. The sun and traffic sounds may be your only clues. You'll get better at sensing your environment the more you practice."

Next, I learned how to find particular storefronts.

"Walk to the corner and turn left without crossing the street. Find the third door on your left."

I did as Lisa said and found the store.

My next challenge was to learn how to ride public transportation. I was once again struck by how different life was for a blind person. Riding public transportation was scary. I hadn't been on a bus in Saint Louis in over twenty-five years—not since I'd made a few trips to the zoo before I'd gotten my driver's license. Since I was blinded, I'd been using taxi cabs and had gotten very comfortable with cab drivers and the great service provided by Saint Louis County Cab. Riding a bus would be completely different.

"When it's time for your final exam," Lisa said, "I'll be dropping you off in downtown Little Rock. I'll give you bus fare, and you'll need to find your way back to Lions World. I'll be waiting there for you, so you'll be all on your own," Lisa said.

"I guess I better learn how to ride a bus," I said, but I was grateful that I would likely be able to continue to use taxi cabs in my real life. Door-to-door service seemed like a luxury compared to having to understand, and be limited by, bus schedules.

We went to the bus stop. "You want bus 62," Lisa said. "You'll have to call the bus company to find out the number of the bus you need to catch for your test. Today we're just going to ride a couple of blocks on bus 62."

"How will I know which one is 62?" I asked.

"When the bus stops, listen for the doors to open. Ask the bus driver, 'Is this number 62?' He'll tell you whether it is or isn't. If it's 62, get in and hand him the fare. Try to sit close to the front and tell the driver the name of the street where you want to get off. He'll let you know when your stop comes up. Bus drivers are generally really good and reliable."

Just then a bus pulled up, and I heard the door open.

"Is this Bus 62?" I shouted at what I believed was the open bus door.

"Yes," was the reply. "Come forward and step in. That'll be twenty-five cents," he said as he tapped the fare box to let me know where it was. I dropped in a quarter. "There's a seat right behind me," he said.

"We want to get off at Main Street," Lisa said.

I was nervous but found my seat.

A few minutes later, the driver announced, "Main Street." I got up and found my way out the front door.

"Thank you," I told the driver. I stepped down to the street and walked forward until I found the curb. Up and onto the sidewalk. I stood there before turning and asked Lisa, "Which way are we going?"

We spent several hours each day walking around downtown and other neighborhoods in Little Rock. On a few rainy mornings, we went to a shopping mall when it first opened. There weren't many other people there at that early hour. The escalators represented both a landmark and another opportunity to learn. Lisa lined me up about ten feet from an escalator and told me to walk forward.

"Feel the floor carefully," she said. The mall floor was very smooth. As I took a few steps, my cane came to a very rough surface that had a metallic sound. I stopped.

"The floor changed," I said.

"That rough surface is the area in front of the escalator. It lets you know that you're close. Take another step or two forward and find the handrail with your left hand," Lisa coached. "Now step onto the escalator while steadying yourself with your left hand."

As I stepped forward, I found the moving escalator and a step rose up under my feet. I was moving up.

"Place your cane tip down a stair or two in front of you so that you can feel where to step off. You should also be able to feel through your left hand when the handrail starts levelling out just before you reach the end," Lisa instructed.

I stumbled a bit at the top but got the picture. Now, I just needed more practice.

———————

In mid-November, my counselor Ray Schaeffer and I agreed that I should finish up at Lions World before Thanksgiving, which meant that the Friday before, I'd be going home for good. I knew I could study and practice Braille forever if I was going to have to read and write it quickly. We all agreed.

I felt I'd learned all that I was going to learn in Little Rock about using a computer, and I made my case. Ray agreed and gave me the name of someone in Saint Louis who could order a laptop and the necessary software and adaptation for me, as well as provide more training as needed.

My last hurdle was to pass the final exam in the O&M Department: the solo bus ride home from downtown Little Rock. Could I do it? I felt pretty good about my skills, but I still got turned around at times. Lisa was often right behind me, and on at least one occasion when she had said to do XYZ and come back to a certain spot to meet her, I'd felt her hand on my shoulder when I started to make a wrong turn. Would she shadow my bus ride? My test was scheduled for Monday during my last week, so I could repeat it if necessary.

During these last couple of weeks, something had either changed or I just became more aware. Diabetes is the largest cause of blindness, and many of the other students at Lions World were diabetic. I'd started to hear ambulances pull up every day—sometimes more than once. Many of the students were experiencing diabetic shock. They would lose energy, sit down somewhere, and no one would know that they were there. When a sighted person finally discovered them, more than orange juice was often necessary and an ambulance was called. I gained a great respect for this disease and was, again, grateful that I was "only" blind. During my last week, the regular whine of ambulances began to make me uncomfortable. No disrespect to the diabetic individuals who were in trouble, but I couldn't wait to get home, away from the sirens for good.

On Monday, Lisa drove me downtown.

"Here's a quarter for the bus. From where we are now, you should walk to your right a block and a half, crossing only one street. Don't cross the second street you come to, but turn right and walk to the bus stop at the end of that block. You are looking for bus number 35. Where will you tell the driver you want to go?"

"Fair Park at Thirtieth."

"Good. The bus is due in fifteen minutes, so get going. I know you'll do fine."

"I'm glad you're sure," I said.

I followed Lisa's directions and was standing where I thought the bus stop was. A bus pulled up, and I felt the burst of air as the door opened.

"Bus 35?" I hollered.

"No, he's the next one," came the reply.

Soon another bus stopped, and that one was mine. I paid my fare and took the first seat on the passenger side, so I could talk with the driver, and we took off.

"Fair Park and Thirtieth," the driver finally announced.

"Are you on the near side of Thirtieth?" I asked.

"Yes, it's still in front of us."

"Thanks," I said as I got off. Now all I had to do was find the corner, get oriented, and turn right. This was the sidewalk at the rear of Lions World, if I hadn't made a mistake.

Down the sidewalk, turn right, and look for the sidewalk to the front door. Just like the first day I'd walked with a cane. Up the front walk to the front door. Down the hallway to the O&M office on the left.

"I made it!" I announced.

"We're busy. We'll be with you in a minute," a voice said.

I thought I'd just accomplished something important, and they didn't seem impressed. I was confused, but then heard Lisa say, "Congratulations Bill. I knew you could do it. We're just messing with you. You did great. You must have caught the first bus and gotten here directly. It's only been forty minutes since I dropped you off."

I had an exit interview with my counselor and another with the psychologist. Those were the last boxes I needed to check. Lisa and I still spent the next three days practicing, and I kept after the Braille and technology lab, but my mind was seriously onto the next phase of my journey: living at home.

CHAPTER
SIXTEEN

Lions World had been a good escape from reality. When I came home to Saint Louis for good, my thoughts turned to my big challenges: establishing a new normal with my children, reestablishing my relationships with friends and family, and going back to work.

I'd spent almost five months being cared for by medical and rehabilitation professionals. Large blocks of my time had been devoted to the structured world of health care and rehabilitation, and everyone agreed that I was doing and learning what I needed to. To a large degree, all I had to do while I was in the hospital and rehab was to take advantage of everything the professionals wanted to do for me and learn the things they wanted me to do for myself. It had been a relief to turn my life over to following directions and learning, even if some people thought I'd jumped in too quickly. Obviously, I had not.

Deep down, I was afraid and uncertain about whether I could make it all work on my own. But I made a decision to keep a smile on my face, maintain an upbeat attitude, continue to do whatever I was presented with, and to trust that I was on the right road to get to where I ultimately wanted to be: back to my personal and professional lives with the fewest limitations.

And now here I was—back home, graduated from Lions World, and released from the Department of Neurosurgery.

Once again, I felt all alone in a strange place: I was blind in the world I used to see and know. The scripted part of my journey was over. Now I had to start walking the walk. I had to start dealing with the world as an independent person, not just on weekend visits home—when much of the weekend was filled with family, friends, my children, and increasingly, Virginia—but I had to do it every single day. No one was going to knock on my door to tell me what to do next. The next move was up to me.

Leisure time was not a big challenge. If I was out with friends and family or Virginia, someone always offered me an elbow. I'd taught them all the sighted guide technique. Many times when we were out, my group would walk off without me, and I'd have to say, "Hey! Could someone give me an elbow?" The response was always the same: "Bill, you do so well, I forgot you were blind." I took that as a compliment.

I was pretty comfortable with my life by now but accepting the new me was hard on some of my friends, as well as my family. They were constantly reminded of what had happened to me. If we wanted to get together, I needed a ride. Everyone readily accepted that, and it always seemed like they took my logistics in stride. Although I'd become attached to my cane, it was a constant, visual reminder to everyone else about what had happened. Most of my friends seemed to be comfortable with the new me when they could see that I'd accepted the change, so they eventually got comfortable too.

Next up, Thanksgiving. My sister called our parents from Chicago to say that Rich would be joining us for Thanksgiving dinner in Saint Louis. *The relationship must be going well,* I thought. At Thanksgiving dinner, they announced that they were engaged to be married and were planning the wedding for the day after Christmas. *Going well, indeed*, I thought.

Rich seemed like a really good guy, and they were obviously happy together. It would be Katherine's first marriage. Out of my tragedy, they had met and were planning a life together. Definitely great news, and the wedding would be a happy event after going through so much turmoil.

Virginia and I were also seeing each other several times each week and were having a lot of fun. She agreed to go to the wedding as my date.

"By the way, my friends call me Ginny," she said at some point.

"I like that," I answered. "I'll have to get used to calling you Ginny," assuming I was now a friend.

We both enjoyed going out to dinner, and she seemed game for anything I wanted to do. One evening at an Italian restaurant, we ordered a bottle of red wine. When eating out, I'd learned to locate my place setting with my hand, and I made sure that my glassware was in its place at one or two o'clock to my plate. I had learned that if I held my hand over where I thought the glasses should be and lowered it until I found them, I'd never knock one over. On this night, the attentive waiter topped off our wine glasses several times. One of these times, he apparently moved my wine glass. So, when I reached for the bread basket, I knocked my wine glass across the table toward Ginny.

"Bill!" she shrieked as it played out in slow motion in front of her. The sheer yellow dress she was wearing was ruined, in spite of the efforts of the waitstaff to blot it with tonic water and dry towels. Ginny remained in good spirits, however, even after the dry cleaner told her they couldn't get the red wine out of her yellow dress. After that, we learned to keep an eye on the waiters to prevent them from moving the glasses on our table—a lesson I had not learned at Lions World but a valuable one in my new world.

Ginny's aunt and cousin owned a well-known fruit orchard in Saint Louis named Eckert's. On a visit there one Saturday, her Aunt Juanita said, "You two seem to be getting that tandem walking down pretty good." And we were. It was easier and seemed a little less impersonal for me to put my hand on her shoulder when we walked together, rather than the sighted guide elbow. We were having fun. She had a knack of giving me a hand when I asked but letting me figure out most things on my own. She didn't have the need to nurse me, unless encouraging my independence was nursing. On the other hand, she made daily living much easier for me by doing a myriad of helpful things, some of which, I'm sure, I was not even aware of. For other things like reading labels, envelopes, etc., I was very aware.

December was a busy month. Ginny and I were together a lot, I was getting some time with my kids, and I spent time with my parents. Also, there were some parties surrounding Katherine and Rich's wedding. Everyone in Saint Louis wanted to meet Rich and, of course, congratulate them both.

One such event was a wedding shower at the home of our old neighbor, Tinker. Also invited were several of Katherine's Saint Louis work and school friends, as well as our parents.

We all enjoyed the food and the happy couple's response to the gifts. At one point, I asked Ginny if she could show me to the bathroom. As we passed through the kitchen, one of Katherine's friends stopped us and introduced herself.

Then she looked at Ginny and asked, "In what capacity are you here tonight?"

"What do you mean?" Ginny said, as confused as I was by the question.

"I mean, are you Bill's nurse, or something more?"

"I'm his date, period," was her firm answer.

As we walked on to the bathroom, we shared that we each thought that was a very strange question.

It was a toss-up which of us was more offended. I guess we had both put our original roles when we met behind us because we'd obviously become a couple. We thought that should be obvious to others as well. It was an inappropriate question, but we've gotten a few laughs when we remember the story.

———■———

Going back to work was the big hurdle in front of me that I would have to do largely on my own. No tagging along with friends or family. No unexpected hand on my shoulder from Lisa. The first step was to visit my office and check that off the list. KPMG occupied the top three floors of a twenty-story office building. Would I be able to find my way through the building lobby to the elevator bank? How would my cane and I do in the lobby, which was usually bustling with people? Could I find the right floor and then my office?

I phoned our administrative assistant. "Kristine, It's Bill Johnson. How are you doing?"

"I'm great. It's so good to hear your voice. How are you?" she said.

"I'm good, and I want to come down there tomorrow. You'll be around, won't you?"

"Of course. We would all love to see you. Do I need to do anything to help you?"

"No, thanks. I'm going to see if I can find my way. Can you transfer me to Vince? I want to let him know I'll be there." Vince Cannella was the Managing Partner of the Saint Louis KPMG office, and he had talked to me earlier to offer support for my return to work.

The next morning, I arranged for a cab to take me to the office. Our building was set back from the street with a small open plaza between two buildings that occupied the same block. One side of the building was right on the sidewalk of the cross street. That's the entrance I wanted. We got off the highway and went a couple of blocks.

"It's the black building on the right. Can you let me out right in front of the revolving door?"

"No problem," the cab driver said. "Are you sure you can't see?"

"I'm sure," I said, but it made me smile.

I found the revolving door and remembered that there was a hinged door just to the right. I felt more comfortable with a regular hinged door. The possibility of getting pinched in a revolving door didn't appeal to me. Plus, it was easier to get squared up perpendicular to a flat door. That was my only hope of finding the elevator without some confusion.

The lobby was wide open with several very large, round planters about three feet high where some sort of tree grew. All I had to do was walk straight about thirty feet through the wide-open lobby and turn right into the hallway with the elevators at exactly the right place. I took about six or eight steps before I hit one of the big planters. *No problem. I'll just go to the right and find the wall that connects to the elevator hallway.*

I found it and waited for an elevator door to open. *Ding!* announced the door opening. At Lions World I'd been taught to pause a minute so the elevator could empty, then go in. My office was on the top floor, and I remembered which button was for the twentieth floor, feeling the Braille beside it to confirm. The door closed, and up I went. *What was this going to be like?* I thought. I hadn't been to my office in over five months.

The elevator door opened, and I heard, "Bill Johnson. It's Kay." Kay was our receptionist and a friend.

"Hey, Kay," I said as I walked out and followed the sound of her voice to her desk.

"How in the world are you, Bill? It's sure good to see you."

"I'm OK. It's been an interesting few months."

"It's not the same around here without you and Tony," she said.

"Yeah. It's terrible about Tony. It will never be the same without him," I said as the conversation quickly turned serious.

"What brings you here?" Kay said cheerfully.

"Just wanted to see if I could get down here on my own. I felt like getting out of the house."

"Well, you are here," she said as she answered her ringing phone.

I turned and found the wall where the elevator doors were and followed them around to the left. At the corner, I turned right and, using my cane, I followed the wall until I came to the next corner. *Diagonal to the left, then follow that wall to my office door*, I thought to myself. Bingo!

I walked around my desk and sat down. The phone on my credenza rang. "Bill, it's Kristine. I heard you were here."

"Yep. Even found my office. And my phone. Thanks for making it ring."

"I'll be right down to say hi."

Kristine came down and took a chair in front of my desk.

"How's everything at KPMG?" I asked.

"Better now, seeing you. I'm the one who took the call from the Atlanta police when they called to get identification for Tony and you. I couldn't believe what they were telling me. You and Tony shot. It didn't make any sense, and it still doesn't."

"No, it doesn't make any sense to me either, but I'm the lucky one. I'm here."

"That's a great attitude. I've heard different stories about your injuries. Can you see anything at all?" she asked.

"Not really. Just a little light, but sometimes that's helpful."

"I'm so sorry. I hope you don't mind me asking," she said.

"I don't mind at all. You can ask me anything you want."

Later, others told me that the Atlanta police had found a business card for either Tony or me and had called our office to notify someone about what had happened. Kristine had answered that call. She was hysterical when she got off the phone, and had run, screaming, up to the twentieth-floor lobby. Word spread quickly through the office, and many people reached out to friends in local news organizations for any update. It was hardly necessary, as our shooting was soon the leading story in local newscasts. At first, Tony and I were both reported to be in critical condition. Then the reports said that I had improved but was blind. Then they reported that Tony had passed. I think these were the outcomes the doctors expected from the beginning, but the reporting apparently emphasized the uncertain drama that played out during the first several days.

Kristine went back to her desk, and I went through the routine I'd developed to orient myself to new spaces. I needed to build a vision in my head of where I was, so I felt around my office. Wall with a picture and door, wall with a white board, glass window on the outside wall, and the wall behind my desk, over the credenza. On and around my desk: stapler, blotter, telephone, coffee cup. *That's important,* I thought.

Stacks of unread trade newspapers and magazines were on my window sill, accumulating there because I'd thought I was going to catch up on my reading someday. My piles were so bad that I'd earned the first monthly Sloppy Office of the Month award the month I went to Atlanta. The prize was a nice pink pig cap that had a snout and curly tail and a recognition plaque. We often had clients visit, and I was on the committee whose job it was to get people to keep their offices neat. I'd volunteered to receive the first month's award since I was on the committee, but the truth was that I was afraid I'd get the award anyway.

Kristine returned and sat down.

"Anything I can help you with?" she asked.

"I guess we can pitch a lot of the paper in here," I said slapping a pile of *Communications Week* and *Network World* newspapers. "It's a relief I don't have to read all these," I joked.

"I can read them to you when you get back," Kristine said, "if you want."

"I think I'm having an epiphany. I've done my job for years without reading all of this. Let's throw it all away, and I'll be caught up. Thanks for the offer to read to me. If we do that, let's read the more current issues."

"Makes sense to me," she said. "So, what are your plans, Bill?"

"I plan to come back to work. I'm not sure how that will go, but I'm going to try to do it, and it seems like the firm will let me give it a try."

"That would be amazing. You can't believe how upset and sad everyone's been. It was so grim around here for at least a month. People will be glad to see you again."

"Thanks," I said. "It's great to see you too. It's hard to believe I'm sitting at my desk again. I'm going to walk over to Vince's office."

"Can I help you?" Kristine asked.

"No. I want to find it on my own."

"Can you come by and say hi before you leave?"

"Sure. I think I can find your desk."

My office was near one corner of this floor, and Vince's office was in the corner directly east of me. I had to head from my office door at a forty-five-degree angle to find the wall back to the lobby. Bingo! I followed the wall down the hallway, where the floor changed from carpet to tile, past Kay the receptionist, and back to carpet.

I continued down a straight hall, past some cubicles I remembered, until there was an opening on my right.

"Bill, it's Debbie. How in the world are you?" she asked. She was Vince Cannella's secretary and sat just outside his door.

"I found my way to your desk, so I guess I'm doing pretty good. Is Vince in?"

"He's expecting you. You can go right in."

I turned right and took a few steps toward his spacious corner office. Vince jumped up to shake my hand and directed me to a chair.

"Bill, the whole incident was terrible. I want you to know what an outpouring of sympathy and support came from the firm when you were shot."

"Thanks. It means a lot to me, but it won't bring Tony back."

"No. It won't. Have you talked with your leadership about coming back?"

"A little. I think they're OK with it."

"If you have any problem, let me know. I really meant what I told you on the phone about finding a job in a support role for the Saint Louis office if your old job doesn't work out.

"Thanks, Vince. It means a lot."

We discussed what I'd been doing the last five months. He seemed genuinely interested in my journey.

After a while, I excused myself and found my way back down the hallway toward my office. When the floor changed from carpet to tile, I said "Hi Kay," as I passed her desk.

"Bill, how did you know I was here?" she asked, sounding confused.

"Magic!" I offered, and continued toward my office. But when I got to the corner, I turned right this time. I used my cane to check the wall on the left and to avoid the cubicles on the right. The walls gave me that highway, just like the grass on either side of the sidewalks. I walked straight to Kristine's desk.

"Hey, Bill," she said.

"I found you," I said.

"You're amazing," she said.

"Thanks. Good to see you. I guess I'll get going. Could you call a cab for me?"

"Sure. County Cab?"

"Yes. Tell them the eleventh street side. I think that door will be easier. And tell them I'm blind, so they need to look for me."

I turned right and went down the other hallway that connected back to the reception area.

Over the next couple of months, I visited the office a couple of times and became more confident in my ability to get around. I was able to find the word processing group on another floor, right past the reproduction department. I generally did OK. I visualized all the hallways, and none of the spaces were so wide open that I would get lost in them.

Except the main lobby. I got to know those big planters too well. They always seemed to be in the way.

——————

A week after Thanksgiving I had an appointment with Greg. Rehab Services had referred me to him to order the talking computer they would provide for me. On one of my weekends home, Greg and I had discussed the particulars of my job and what kinds of things I'd need my computer to do. From that conversation, Greg had ordered a Toshiba laptop with the voice card soldered inside and the adaptive program installed. He brought the computer with him that day.

"Here you are," he said as he handed me the laptop.

"It's not very heavy," I said.

"Set it in front of you and see if you can open it."

I felt around the outside edges until I found something that felt like a release button.

"Good job. Now, put your fingers on the keyboard, and see what you think."

"It feels nice," I said. "Little bumps on the f and j, so I can find the starting position—just like the IBMs at Lions World."

"I'll show you how the other keys are laid out and give you the first lesson in WordPerfect, your word processing program."

Greg spent several hours reviewing what I had learned at Lions World and teaching me new shortcuts to create new documents, save documents, and retrieve saved documents. Seemed very easy. He also loaded a couple of files on the hard drive that contained the directions and other tips.

"This voice is pretty mechanical sounding, but I guess I'll get used to it," I said.

"You'll get accustomed to it quickly, and you may even want to turn up the speed as you start to understand it better."

Finally. Here was a real solution to that information and note storage problem I'd encountered my first week home. This was much more sophisticated than the dictation machine with messages and information all stacked sequentially on the same audio tape. Now that I knew how to use the computer, I started keeping every telephone number and address in a WordPerfect document named *Telephone*. Pretty simple, but it worked. Same thing with keeping a calendar—another document named *Calendar*.

I soon had other files and notes about various things, and I not only became proficient with creating and manipulating files, I became dependent on this new tool. All the little notes I used to keep on yellow note pads now were put at the beginning of the *Telephone* document, so I bumped right into my to-do list every time I opened that document. I could do enough with the computer that note taking, writing, and staying organized shouldn't prevent me from doing my job. This computer allowed me to feel like a capable, knowledgeable person who could keep track of his life and take care of business. One more step on my journey.

I spent my days getting my house and my life more streamlined and developing systems for the new me. I hired a contractor to build the deck that I'd planned to build myself. I got my Mom to go through every item in my kitchen with me. Anything I didn't need for the small list of things I thought I'd try to cook was discarded. No more cupboard full of boxes and cans with no identity. I put a rubber band around a few things to differentiate them. Lions World had shown me how I could type Braille labels on magnetic Dymo label tape if I wanted to identify a lot of cans of different things, but, for now, one rubber band for pork and beans, 2 rubber bands for tomato sauce, etc.

My mail collected in the dining room, and I'd accost my visitors to tell me what the pieces were. Most was junk mail or magazines, and they hit the trash can. Mom still got the bills to pay. My wardrobe had always tended toward blue jeans and polo shirts. I didn't own anything that wouldn't go with anything else, so matching clothes to wear wasn't a problem. Dress clothes were even simpler: suits and blue or white shirts.

Engaging my children on their visits was another challenge. I used to read them bedtime stories, *Goodnight Moon* being a favorite. I discovered that The National Library Service for the Blind and Physically Disabled had Braille books, in addition to books on tape. They even had children's books, so I ordered some. I got a kick out of being able to read bedtime stories to them again, no matter how slow my reading was. I didn't hear any complaints, but before long, Chris was reading faster than me. But it's the experience and memory of reading bedtime stories together that's important, right? Not how fast the parent reads.

We continued to play Keep the Kids Out of the Kitchen, and we always ended up laughing. Chris was obsessed with Legos, and I found that I could help him. Identifying the different pieces by feel was not too difficult, and it was fun.

Cooking for them wasn't hard either because their demands were not great. Breakfast—including scrambled eggs and bacon—wasn't too tough. Both kids carried on a family tradition of loving tuna salad sandwiches—it had to be Bumble Bee Albacore and real mayonnaise—and I could make them in my sleep. Kelly went through phases during her early years when she wanted to eat the same thing for dinner for months at a time. I remember macaroni and cheese, toasted ravioli, and chicken tenders. During the first months, it was linguine with olive oil and butter sauce with a little parmesan cheese. Chris would eat anything, so I often made linguine with onion, peppers, and mushrooms in an oil and butter garlic sauce. I just separated the sauce for Kelly. When I made something that required measurements, I would get Chris's help to find the right spot on the measuring cup. We made it a group effort, and it was fun. Everyone was happy, and no one starved.

One regular pleasure was going out to dinner at Algonquin Country Club with Mom and Dad. Dad had joined the club in the early 1980s when he retired from Southwestern Bell, and he'd planned to spend his retirement on the golf course. It was all working out as he'd planned. He had a number of great friends who also enjoyed golf and gin rummy. I'd gotten to know most of them over the years, and I knew how supportive they were of both Mom and Dad after my shooting.

One evening at dinner, Dad said, "Bill, I'm just amazed at how you have handled this and how you carry on your life."

"Thanks," I said. "What choice did I have? I sure don't want to sit around my house all day and do nothing. I want to keep doing everything I can."

"Well, not everyone would feel that way, so I congratulate you. I've known other people who were blind, and you've already developed the ability to look people in the eye, just like they did. How do you do that?"

"I haven't really thought about that," I said. "I guess I can hear where you are, and since your eyes are above your mouth, I look there."

My friends all learned little lessons about the new me, too. One night, my friend Mark came over to help me hook up a stereo pre-amp I wanted to try out. When he had it in place, he said, "There, it fits right in the cabinet where the old one was."

"Let me see it," I said, meaning I wanted to feel it. As I stood up, my foot hit something slightly heavy. I reached over and uprighted it. "Was that your beer?" I asked.

"Oops. Yeah. I guess I shouldn't leave beers around on the floor."

"A waste of good beer," I said, and we both laughed.

I'd explored my neighborhood with my cane a little during the warm fall weekends when I'd come home from Lions World. Walking around the block was doable, but still not optimum, because two sides of the block didn't have sidewalks. One day, I decided to try to walk up to the Old Orchard business district in Webster Groves, the suburb I lived in.

Getting there was complicated by two things. There was an interstate highway between my house and the business district, and there were two different streets I could take to walk the five or six blocks north to get close to the highway overpass. The busier of the two streets didn't have a continuous sidewalk. The other choice was my own street, which seemed the safest option.

I decided to see how far I could get. I was already familiar with the first couple of blocks. Go down my driveway, turn left, and make my way up the block with no sidewalk. Cross the street to find the sidewalk. Cross the next street, and I should have sidewalk up to the point that the interstate highway had, many years ago, cut off this street. I crossed East Jackson and was into new territory. I knew that at some point, I'd need to turn right for one block to catch the busy road. I thought I remembered that I could cross that last street and find a sidewalk on the far side, but there was no forward path. Just a right turn.

After a couple of blocks, I encountered a kind of gravelly mess. Was it a driveway or street repair? I tried to walk straight across it. Then tried to find the street on my left. I forgot to remember Lisa's advice, "When you become unsure of what's going on, stop and think. What clues do you have? Stand still."

I continued to flail around and soon found a concrete path. My cane hit a barrier that turned out to be someone's front porch. Wrong direction, but now I was reoriented. I turned around and headed toward the street. When I found the sidewalk, I turned right, and soon found the gravel, but this time I walked straight across to pick up the sidewalk again.

A little later, it felt like the sidewalk was bending around a bit to the right. I pictured the rounded corner at the last cross street—the one I was looking for. I thought I was following the curve around, when I heard, "Hello. Can I help you?"

"Ah, hello. Am I on the sidewalk?"

"No. You just walked up my driveway."

"Oops. Sorry about that," I said.

"No problem."

I turned around and made my way back to the sidewalk. This time, I turned left and headed for home. Enough exploring for one day.

———■———

As my new deck was taking shape, I decided to get a new gas grill to put on it. I did a little shopping by phone and decided to visit the Laclede Gas appliance store downtown.

"Ginny, could you take me on an errand?" I asked.

"Sure. Maybe you'll buy me lunch while we're downtown?"

We went in the store and I carefully felt several models they sold. I ordered a large two-burner model with a pedestal base. I was planning to hook it up to natural gas. They said that it would be delivered in about a week, and it would need to be assembled.

A week later, the doorbell rang.

"Hello, can I help you?" I asked.

"UPS. I've got a large box. Where should I put it?"

"Just inside the door here. I'll take it from there," I said.

I assumed it was the new grill, and my curiosity got the best of me. I pushed the box back to the kitchen and sliced the tape, so I could open the box. Yep. That's what it was. The grill. The first thing I felt in the box was the lid. I lifted it out and felt inside. There were several bags of parts, some with small items, and a couple with larger shapes that felt like the handle and knobs. I put the lid back in the box and went back to whatever I'd been doing when the doorbell rang.

After lunch, I bumped into the UPS box, reminding me that the grill was there. *I should be able to put that together,* I thought to myself. *If I'm really careful with the small parts, someone else can finish it if I can't.* I went down to the basement and found a couple of screwdrivers and a ratchet set and brought them upstairs. Next, I found a Tupperware container to put the bag of small parts into so that I wouldn't lose them.

Again, I took the lid out of the box and set it aside. Then I started exploring the larger bagged items. *Two knobs, probably to slide on the stems of the valves. The handle for the top. I'll need to find the nut for the inside of the handle. Here's the upright post and the patio base that it fits into.* I felt carefully on the base and the post for pre-drilled screw or bolt holes. The base had one hole that would fit a bolt to tighten onto the post. I found a similar hole on the bottom of the grill itself where it mounted on the post. *Here's a piece of paper. Probably the directions. That's worthless!*

I dumped out the bag of smaller items into my Tupperware. I found one larger nut which fit onto the handle on the lid, then felt around for a washer or split washer the same size and located it. The next two biggest things were bolts. I checked to see if they would thread into the holes where the post seated on the base and the grill. They did, so I started them in the threads and mounted the post on the base.

There were six smaller screws with matching lock washers. I figured out that they held the burner assembly in place. Then I mounted the grill on the base, the burner into the grill, and installed the handle and knobs. After tightening up all the bolts, I raised and lowered the lid. *That seems like a barbeque grill,* I thought. And I had no pieces left over. That's always a good sign! I set the grill against the door to the deck and carried the box and tools down to the basement.

The next time Ginny was over, she saw it and said, "Oh, your grill came. Did your Dad put it together for you?"

"No, I got bored, and did it myself."

"Who read you the directions?"

"I don't need no stinkin' directions," I joked. "I just felt all of the pieces. I knew what it was supposed to look like, so I just put it all together."

"Wow. I'm not sure I could put it together using the directions," she said, with a hint of marvel in her voice.

While I was proud of myself for accomplishing this, I was acutely aware that there were permanent losses in my life, particularly in terms of freedom and privacy. I'd never again to be able to drive a car, to go to the store on a whim to get a bag of potato chips for a snack. If I wanted to go somewhere, I had to beg a ride, walk, or wait, sometimes for up to an hour, for a cab to pick me up—if they came at all. So much time wasted waiting, waiting, waiting. Everything took more time that it did before, from showering and dressing to cooking my meals. The daily routine of living that had been quick and easy before was now long and laborious. I'd never play racquetball again, never read my own mail, never balance my own checkbook, never enjoy the artwork in my home. And these things would never change. I had to adapt and accept.

———————

Katherine's wedding day was set for the day after Christmas, and it finally arrived. It was a simple ceremony at the country club with a great meal afterward.

"Bill, I'd be honored if you'd be my best man," Rich said.

"Of course. It would be my pleasure. What do I need to do?"

"Hold onto the ring until I need it, and make a few remarks at the wedding if you want."

"I might not be the best one to keep track of the ring, but I'll do my best," I joked.

The whole event went off as planned, and I didn't lose the ring. Katherine seemed really happy and was thrilled about her plans to move to Atlanta to continue her legal career remotely.

Many of the guests were my parents' friends. They'd all heard about what had happened to me, and I got many good wishes and congratulations from people I'd known for twenty-five or thirty years.

One of our closest family friends, Parker said, "Well, Johnson, you finally got your sister married off, but did you really have to go to such lengths to make it happen?"

"It was a tough assignment," I laughed.

There was much joy in my life but also some sadness. Young kids often don't want to attract extra attention, especially related to their parents—and I had young kids. Having a blind parent definitely attracted attention. When I visited their school or went to their soccer games, I'd ask, "Could one of you give me a hand?"

"Kelly, you get Dad," Chris would say.

"No, Chris. It's your turn," Kelly would reply as Chris walked away.

"Oh, all right."

I tried to remember how I felt when I was their age and not to take it personally, but these conversations always hurt me. I tried to never let it show and thought of better ways to ask for their help.

CHAPTER
SEVENTEEN

During my junior year of college in Lawrence, Kansas, three of my fraternity brothers and I squeezed into a 1966 Mustang and took off to go skiing. One of them, J. D., had skied the previous winter, and he assured us that it was easy to learn to ski. He said he would teach us. Why not give it a shot?

I hadn't driven much west of Topeka, which was relatively close to Lawrence, and was unprepared for the long, flat expanse of Kansas and eastern Colorado. As we drove, the roads became quite snow packed and slippery. It was amazing how you could see the silos raising up off the plains to announce the presence of a town from such a long distance. On subsequent ski trips, the lights from Friday night high school football stadiums lit up the night and announced the next town, in the same way the silos did during the day. Farmers' fields were occasionally broken by small towns that I recognized as home to friends I'd met in college. I wondered what it would've been like to grow up in a farm town rather than suburban Saint Louis.

After my junior year in high school, I'd worked one glorious summer at a riding camp in the mountains above Boulder. I loved that summer and the mountains, but I'd never seen them in winter. As we entered Denver, I was struck with the enormity of the Rockies as they rose west of town. First, we saw them from a distance, then all of a sudden, the whole windshield was filled up with the mountains—dashboard to roof line.

For a Midwest guy, the mountains never ceased to overwhelm me. I was excited as we approached, even knowing that we had a few more hours to drive. This was before the Eisenhower tunnel made getting through the highest mountain easier. We drove toward Loveland Pass filled with snow-packed roads and extreme switchbacks as the road went up, up, up. I don't know if it was designated as Interstate 70, but it was the continuation of I-70 through Missouri, Kansas, Colorado, and up and over the continental divide—a two-lane switch-back road that kept going up and switching back. The tires spun at times in the hard pack, and signs announced that chains might be required in order to get over the top.

"I've got some in the trunk," J. D. said as we kept driving. Occasionally, we'd pass stalled cars that had been nearly covered up by the spray of the snow plow. I'd never seen snow plows like these. Besides scraping the roadway, some had vertical scrapers with large screw mechanisms on the curb side of the plow. They chew into the snow pack as it encroaches into the road from the outsides, and shoot the snow up and back, away from the road. In doing so, these trucks had created a ten- or twelve-foot wall of snow on the side of the road. It felt like driving through a tunnel.

It was snowing heavily as we passed cars that had stopped and were spinning their tires. Eventually we got to the summit of Loveland Pass. Success. But now we had to go down several thousand feet. Still the same snow packed roads, but gravity accelerated us rather than holding us back. A touch of the brakes caused the car to swerve as we sped down the hill; downshift to second gear. At least we had a stick shift. Runaway truck ramps were off to the right at the bottom of long hills. What was this all about? We certainly didn't have these in Missouri.

We made it into Summit County and found our motel in Loveland. This was low-budget skiing. Four to a room. I'd bought the cheapest ski jacket and gloves that I could find, and J. D. said we should spray our blue jeans with Scotchguard to keep them dry. That and long johns were going to be my ski wear. Very stylish!

We went into the old town of Breckenridge to explore. J. D. recommended a local hang-out called the All American Bar. It suited us well, and they even had a foosball table. We drank a few beers and played foosball until it was time to go to bed.

The next morning, we woke early. We put on all the layers of warm clothing. We had and lots of Scotchguard. The room reeked of it when we left. Following breakfast, we drove to the Breckenridge ski area. The first order of business was to rent equipment.

Since it was my first time on skis, they gave me pretty short skis, along with poles and boots. We put on our boots and stored our street shoes in the rental shop.

"These boots hurt," I said.

"They'll feel better as the day goes on," the rental guy said.

Outside, J. D. showed us how to lay our skis on the ground and step over them, so we could click into our bindings. Even with two ski poles to support myself, it was pretty awkward trying to stay balanced with my feet on these four-foot skis.

"Am I crazy to do this?" I asked J. D.

"Just give it three days and you'll love it," he replied. "Don't worry about how you feel the first day."

We shuffled off to the ski lift which served the bunny hill. I watched as the pairs of people in front of me shuffled forward. When it came their turn to board the lift, they shuffled out, made a hard left without crossing and tripping on each other's skis, moved another step or two, and squatted a bit to prepare for the chair to come up from behind. Most skiers made this look easy, but I could see that moving into position offered little margin for error because the chair was coming from behind on its own schedule. You had to be ready when your chair came.

"OK," the lift worker said, and J. D. and I shuffled forward, hard left up to the line, and stopped. "Chair!" the lift worker said as we sat.

"When we get to the top, you need to ski away from the lift in a snow plow," J. D. said.

We had practiced the snow plow on the littlest bit of slope outside the lift, so I had a vague idea what was in store for me at the top. As we neared the end of the lift, the ground came up and met the bottom of our skis. As we moved closer to the exit ramp, I stood up and got into my snow plow stance. Down the ramp, I needed to turn to the left. As I tried to follow left, I wiped out and one of my skis was ripped off. I heard the pitch of the lift lower as the operator slowed it down so that other skiers wouldn't unload on top of me. I scrambled to my feet and tried to get my ski back onto my boot. It seemed like the whole resort was waiting on me to get out of the way as I learned that I needed to release the binding, and step into it to get the ski attached to the boot again. Finally done, I shuffled forward to the top of the slope.

Even though this was the bunny hill, I was suddenly struck with the thought that this was all a mistake. People were everywhere, moving in all directions, and it seemed steep to me. Worse, the skis didn't have a brake or a steering wheel. J. D. demonstrated how to traverse the slope from left to right.

"When you get close to the side, transfer your weight to the outside, or right, ski. That should cause you to turn left," he said, and demonstrated.

I started traversing from the left side to the right in my snow plow "V." As I traversed, pushing on my right ski cause me to turn a bit downhill and gain speed, putting weight on the left ski steered me back into the hill and slowed me down. So far, so good. As I neared the right edge of the slope, I started turning into a sharp left turn to begin my right-to-left traverse. *Weight on the right ski. Turning left. Oh my God! I'm pointed straight down the hill and gaining speed! Keep weight on the right ski and start turning into the hill to lose the speed.* Was this fun? It was mostly scary.

I went back across to the left and repeated the turn to the right this time. Same sensation of too much speed and no control. And this was only the bunny hill!

I spent a good part of that morning on my butt on the bunny hill. Fortunately, the Scotchguard was working and my jeans weren't wet. Given my total lack of ability to stop or turn quickly, and the other skiers having the same skill level, I fell down due to collisions, to avoid collisions, and for no apparent reason. But somehow, it seemed kind of fun.

J. D. went off to ski by himself while the rest of us went up and down on this easy hill. One of our friends, John, showed little aptitude for the cold or athletic endeavors, and he quickly went inside to get warm and drink beer.

At lunchtime we all met back up, and J. D. announced, "It's time to go to the top. You've learned to stop and turn."

I had? I thought, but off we went to another lift.

The rest of that day and the next I tried to negotiate slightly steeper terrain. It was a matter of gaining confidence in my ability to turn and stop on increasingly steep runs. It wasn't very pretty, and the snow plow turns and stops were tough on my legs, but it was a little less scary and a lot more fun.

At one steep spot above the lift, there wasn't enough room to traverse. The only way down was straight down the hill, with room to slow down where it flattened out at the bottom. I scooted up to the edge of the drop-off and looked over. Wow. J. D. went and I followed him. It was too fast and icy to snow plow. My skis seemed to rotate slightly, relative to straight ahead. The speed was exhilarating, and the whole sensation was more than a little scary.

"Let's do that again!" I said when we got to the lift line.

Toward the end of the second day, I was making my slow traverse when "Ooph!" and I was knocked to the ground.

"Are you OK?" a voice said. "I couldn't stop," he said.

"I'm OK." I said as I got to my feet. "No problem."

"I'm so sorry. Are you sure you're OK?"

"I'm fine," I said as we both put on our skis and went our separate ways.

As I skied a little more, my right knee felt cold. When I looked down, I saw that my blue jeans were cut open, and that my long johns were red with blood. The other guy's ski had apparently sliced through my pants and into my leg. It was late in the day, so I went into the bar to inspect my knee and wait for my buddies. I got a couple of band aids from the ski patrol, but that wasn't the end of it.

"You need stitches," they said. "There's a clinic in the nearby town of Frisco."

My friends showed up shortly, and we turned in our skis. We'd been talking about going to Vail the next day to check out a different resort. I showed them my knee and said I needed to get some stitches on the way back to the motel. So, we stopped at the clinic.

"How did this happen?" the doctor asked.

"Somebody skied into me at Breckenridge."

"Let's take a look at it," she said as she cleaned it up. "I think a few stitches should take care of this, but you have to promise you won't ski tomorrow. That would tear the stitches out. When are you going home?"

"We have one more day," I said.

"Promise me you won't ski, or I won't stitch it up," she said.

"OK. I'll sit in the bar tomorrow," I told her as she got out her needle and suture material.

Next day, we took off for Vail. "Should we take your skis?" J. D. asked.

"Hell yes! I'm going to ski," I said. I hoped my knee wouldn't open back up and bleed, but I wasn't going to miss a day of skiing over it. This was fun.

Compared to Breckenridge, Vail was huge. We skied all day. My stitches ripped out almost immediately, and my blue jeans developed a dark spot around my knee. Toward the end of the day, I was very tired as we tried to find our way down. We avoided one difficult-looking blue run by following a wide road off to the right. It was going well, but after about 100 yards, the road ended in a run called "Look Ma." The sign showed a black diamond. "Look Ma" had moguls the size of Volkswagens, was steeper than anything we'd yet attempted, and there was no other way down. I was nowhere near capable of skiing down this run even if I were fresh, and at the end of the day, I was whipped.

"Here goes," I said. After about two turns I was going too fast and launched off a mogul onto my back. I slid about forty feet to a stop and considered my options. Stand on this cliff and try to put my skis back on and ski down? Or hug my skis to my chest and slide down the rest of "Look Ma" on my butt. My butt got pretty wet. Apparently the Scotch-guard was failing, but I made it to the bottom.

J. D.'s three-day theory was right. We'd had a great day, and I was hooked on skiing.

For the next several years, I skied at least once per year. Twice in Aspen and once at Steamboat with a couple of friends from high school. My skiing never got too pretty. I thought the object was to go as fast as I could until I crashed. Then I got up and did it again, while getting more comfortable on steeper and more difficult runs. I never took a lesson, but I got pretty comfortable that I could negotiate much of the mountain safely, if not with the best form.

Exploring the bars in the ski towns was always part of the attraction of these trips. On one memorable trip to Aspen, we got tickets to a Nitty Gritty Dirt Band show at the Aspen Inn.

Steve Martin was the opening act—before anyone had heard of him. He did the whole arrow through the head bit and made animals out of balloons. We had tickets in the back for the first show. Steve Martin was hilarious, and Nitty Gritty was one of my favorite bands at the time. After the first show, J.D. said, "Let's move up to the front row and see if we can stay for the second show." We did.

The Aspen Inn was a night club with cocktail tables and waiter service. Being in the front row meant that our table was up against the stage, which was only about three feet off the floor. It turned out that The Nitty Gritty Dirt Band lived in Aspen, and this was their last night at home before going out on the road. They put everything they had into that show. We enjoyed the drinks and the music, and we quickly progressed to taking tequila shots. We offered some shots to the band, and they joined us. Around midnight, they announced that someone else was going to join them. They apologized for including a comedian in their act but assured the audience that Steve Martin could actually play the banjo. As far as I could tell, he seemed to do fine.

Several songs later, the lead singer said "There's another guy who wants to play with us. We don't really like his style of music, so we'll make him play ours." John Denver walked out on stage, and they jammed until about two in the morning. We were all a little rough when the alarm went off too early the next day, reminding us we were there to ski.

———

In December 1972, I graduated college with a degree in psychology, and I decided to move to Aspen for the rest of the ski season. I was dating a girl named Katie at the time, and my plan was that she and I would go skiing for a week. When she had to go back to college, I'd stay and ski every day. That week was wonderful, and while Katie was still there, I found a sleeping dorm to stay in and a bus boy job at the Holiday Inn at the base of Buttermilk-Tiehack. Other than the fact that I'd pictured myself as a stud bartender living in a luxurious Aspen condo, it seemed like I was ready to be a ski bum. I liked the sound of that.

What could possibly go wrong? I had to report to work at 5:00 a.m. on five mornings per week to work the breakfast shift. *Crappy hours*, I thought. *Maybe that's why this job was open.* I spent a good chunk of my small savings on a pair of skis, figuring that I'd be skiing so much that I'd save a bunch on rentals. I did ski several days that first week.

And then I got my paycheck. I'd hoped for more. I paid for a week at the sleeping dorm and had very little left. It quickly became apparent that I couldn't live the life I'd pictured, skiing and partying. I stuck it out for a couple of months, never able to find a better job. I got in some more skiing, though not as much as I'd hoped, and continued to fall in love with Aspen.

I was not quite living the life I'd pictured, and I missed Katie.

By late March I was back in Lawrence, with no particular direction, hoping to pick up the relationship where we had left off.

My psychology degree qualified me to drive a fork lift at a Stokely VanCamp warehouse and not much else. I loved driving the fork lift, but I couldn't picture myself working in the warehouse long-term. So that spring I took the GRE exam, so I could get into business school to pursue an MBA.

The relationship with Katie was soon over, but not before she surprised me with an Irish Setter puppy. She and I had been together when my last dog was hit by a car, and it was a thoughtful gift. I named her Canyon, after a dog I'd met at the sleeping dorm in Aspen.

By the time I graduated with an MBA, I'd probably gone on five ski trips, each between three and six days. In total, I'd had about thirty days of skiing. Between 1974 and 1992, I only had one other ski trip to Aspen, where I skied another four or five days.

I had, however, become very familiar with two ski areas in Aspen: Buttermilk and Aspen Highlands. At one of them, I'd seen a blind skier.

CHAPTER
EIGHTEEN

I'd enjoyed skiing eighteen years earlier, but I never got very good at it. I remembered that in Aspen, I'd seen that skier wearing an orange bib that said BLIND SKIER. Another person had skied with him, also wearing an orange bib. That's all I could remember, but I got on the phone with the Aspen Ski Corporation to figure out who I needed to talk to about skiing again.

I was referred to a disabled skier program at Snowmass, just outside of Aspen. They referred me to Peter Manes who ran the BOLD program. BOLD stood for Blind Outdoor Leisure Development. Peter was a great guy.

After telling him my story, I asked, "Do you think I can do this?"

"Why not?" he said. "As long as your doctor says it's OK. When do you want to come out?"

Before I knew it, I'd made plans to go skiing in mid-February. Peter recommended a place to stay called the Mountain House.

"They offer a discount to blind skiers, and the manager, Sid, will be your guide at least one of the days."

"OK. I'll see you when I get there." That was simple.

The next time I saw Ginny, I asked "Would you like to go skiing with me?"

"Sure," she said, game for anything. "When do you want to go?"

I gave her the dates and asked, "Do you know how to ski?"

"I skied some when my daughter was in college," she said, "but that was twenty years ago, and I wasn't all that good then."

"But that's a start," I said. "We ought to have a blast."

"I know you've been talking about this," she said, "but are you actually going to ski?"

"I've talked to the right people, and I don't see why I shouldn't try it."

February arrived, and we flew to Denver. Ginny drove the rental car to Aspen. There was a lot of snow that year, particularly while we were driving. Leaving Denver, I remembered the first, lower, climb up the mountain. After some driving, Ginny said "We are coming to the Eisenhower Tunnel.

"Tell me when we enter it," I said.

"We are entering it now."

We drove straight for some time, until Ginny announced, "We are leaving the tunnel now."

None of the exaggerated switchbacks, or the runaway truck lanes. The tunnel went under it all and made that portion much easier than I remembered. But forty-five minutes later, getting over Vail Pass was a bit harrowing for Ginny. She described seeing a tractor-trailer jackknife ahead of us. We weren't close enough to be involved, but did we get stuck in traffic. It took about four hours to get to Aspen, but finally, Ginny and I arrived at the Mountain House.

"Feel this," Ginny said as she put my hand on the top of a snowdrift. The sidewalk leading to the front door had been cleared, but the snow was piled about six feet high on each side. It sparked a memory of the tunnel-like path that those snow plows created on the old Loveland Pass.

Earlier that day I'd called Sid, the manager, and asked if there was any way he could put a red rose in our room, since we were arriving on Valentine's Day. Sid made it happen.

"Is that rose for me?" Ginny asked.

"Who else? Happy Valentine's Day, Ginny." We were off to a great start.

My next call was to Peter, who ran the BOLD program.

"Show up at Buttermilk Ski School tomorrow morning at 8:00," he said. "You'll have a lesson with Muriel to get started, and you'll ski with her the first day."

Oddly, this would be my first actual ski lesson. "I'll be there," I said.

"You can rent skis right there at Buttermilk," Peter added. "That way if you need to change to shorter or longer skis during the day, you can."

That evening, Ginny and I went out to explore the town of Aspen. I remembered the names of the streets and a few of the bars and restaurants, but much had changed. A new hotel was built at the base of Aspen Mountain where the Aspen Inn had once been, and many of the businesses were new. We couldn't find the old sleeping dorm where I'd stayed twenty years earlier, but that was OK because it wasn't such a fond memory. The old Holiday Inn at the base of Buttermilk was still there, but it had changed names. I planned to check it out some day.

We found a casual place for Valentine's Day dinner, Little Annie's. It became a favorite of ours for their fried clams and Fat Tire beer.

The Mountain House provided a good hot breakfast, served family style in their dining room. Sid, the manager, came in and out as everyone got their day started. The talk was all about snow conditions and skiing. What a fun atmosphere! The other guests were nice and had come from all over the country.

"What are you two doing today?" a man asked Ginny and I, presumably looking at my white cane.

"Buttermilk for lessons. It will be my first day skiing blind, and Ginny is getting a lesson to brush up on her skills."

"Oh, you mean that you can ski?" he asked.

"I'll find out today. I have in the past, but I was only blinded last summer, so this will be a new experience."

"I'm amazed," he said. "How does that work?"

"Other than knowing that someone skis behind me, I'm not sure. Ask me tomorrow, and I'll tell you more."

"You are braver than I am," he said laughing.

We made it to Buttermilk and found Muriel. Since Ginny had signed up for her own lessons, we went our separate ways.

Muriel had a hint of an accent that was very charming. "I'm from Switzerland and have worked with blind skiers for twenty-five years," she said.

"Do you think I can do it?" I asked.

"Absolutely." She, Peter, and Sid had all been so positive. It was a welcome change from all the negativity I'd heard from my roommate in Arkansas and at that one meeting at work.

"Now, tell me, how well did you ski the last time you went?" Muriel asked.

"I got around OK, but I probably didn't look very good."

"Did you snow plow?" she asked.

"Mostly, but I tried to keep my skis more together. I could do hockey stops, rather than snow plow stops. I've skied most of this mountain and remember some of the runs."

"Did you ski mostly beginner—green—or intermediate—blue—runs?" Muriel asked.

"Both. Maybe not so good on the more difficult blues."

"We'll start from the beginning," she said, "and you'll do great."

"So, tell me how this works," I said.

"I'll ski behind you, and call out commands like *left, right, or stop*," she said.

"Don't you use radio headsets?" I asked.

"We don't. Even with more advanced skiers, we ski close enough for the blind skier to hear our commands. Then it's up to me to be close enough for you to hear me," Muriel said. "We aren't comfortable with the reliability of the two-way radios on the market. The last thing we want is to have an unreliable communication link between us. There will be times when I need you to react to my command immediately, and a burst of static at that moment would not be good."

"I guess you must ski pretty close to me," I said.

"With advanced skiers, we ski as close to the tails of your skis as we can, sometimes making our turns in the same path as you. Today, you won't be skiing that fast, so I'll just stay above you on the hill and give you some room," she said. "I may also say hold or traverse when I want you to keep going without turning. We need to agree on what I'll say if you're in danger, and I want you to fall down."

"Really?" I said as I pictured various threatening situations—running into trees, skiers, or other objects.

"If you hear me say *crush*, you should stop and fall down immediately. Got it?" she said.

"Got it."

We went to the ski rental shop to get me set up with skis, boots, and poles. Oh, the feel of rental ski boots. They're not very comfortable, but your foot seems to mold to the shape of the boot, or vice versa, and before too long they're manageable. But walking in ski boots with their inflexible ankle made me land each step on my heel. The possibility of slipping was ever present. When I got my skis and poles for the day, Muriel offered me her elbow, and we went outside.

"I'll help you get your skis on," she said. "Here are your poles. Just stand here with your legs apart, and steady yourself with the poles. I'll put your skis on the snow. Now, lift up your right foot. Point your toe down and feel for the toe piece on the binding. Here, I'll help you," she said as she directed my boot. "Now move your heel to the right. Perfect. Now step down."

Click! the binding responded as I was locked in. We got the other ski on, and I stood there with my pole tips on the ground, sliding my skis forward and backward.

"It feels kind of slippery," I said.

"Next we need to put this orange ski bib on you. It says *Blind Skier* in large black letters on an orange background. It should tell people to stay away from us, but it seems they often want to get closer to read it. But, that's what we have to wear. I wear one that says *Blind Guide*. I'll put it over your head. Then you can feel two strings on each side and tie them together, at your waist. There, perfect. You look like a skier!" Muriel said.

"Let's go. I'll come up on your left and grab your pole," she said as her hand came up below mine. "I'll direct you with your pole and give some descriptions as we get over to the bunny hill. Now shuffle forward."

We soon arrived at the bunny hill. I'd seen it but had never skied on it. I thought I was much too good of a skier—and way too cool—to be seen on the bunny hill. *Ski bunny* is not a particularly complimentary term around skiers. It's a reference to women who look good in their expensive ski gear around the fireplace at the lodge or at the bar, but aren't very good skiers. The bunny hill was little more than the grade that my house was on, but it was definitely where my new skiing experience needed to start. Two steps backwards before I could take a step forward.

As we stood at the top, Muriel said "The slope is directly to your left. When I tell you to go, turn your skis a little to your left and start traversing across the slope. Listen for me to call a right turn, then do it. Let's see how it goes. Point your skis a little left and push off."

I moved forward. It felt a little unsteady, but not so bad.

"Right turn," Muriel said, reminding me that I needed to listen for her. I was going so slow that all I could muster was a snowplow turn.

"Good" Muriel said. "Hold it, hold it, hold it . . . left turn," she said. I'd picked up a little bit of speed in the traverse but made another snowplow turn. As my skis got halfway through the turn and pointed down the hill, I remembered the terror I'd felt learning to do the same thing at Breckenridge twenty years earlier. Like then, I knew that if I just held on to the turn, my skis would eventually turn across the hill, and I'd regain control of my speed. We continued to the bottom, stopping a couple of times to prove to both of us that I could stop.

"Now we'll get on the lift to go back up. I'll take your pole," Muriel said as her hand came up under my left hand and grabbed my pole. "Do you remember what lift lines look like?" she asked.

"Yes. There's a lot of back and forth like the security line at the airport."

"Yes. We'll go through the line. Then we'll stop just before it's our time to get on the lift. I'll say stop here, then when the chair in front of us passes, I'll say step forward. When we get to the right spot, I'll say stop. I'll count down 3-2-1 as the chair approaches us. Reach down behind you with your left hand for the seat to come up from behind and sit down."

We moved through the lift line and through the points she had described. I had memories of the lift speeding along at a brisk pace and having to rush to get in front of it, but Muriel stayed cool, and we got on without incident.

"When we get to the top, I'll say tips up, and you'll feel the snow hit the bottom of your skis. Did you remember that there's a short, steep hill coming off of these lifts?" she asked.

"Yes."

"Put both of your poles in your right hand, and your left hand on my forearm when we get off. Then just ski along beside me until we come to a stop. We'll go slightly to our right when we get off. Tips up."

I lifted my tips and waited for the snow to come up to meet my skis.

"3, 2, 1, stand up," Muriel said, and we accelerated down the ramp. I could feel her directing me to the right, where we came to a stop.

"That was exciting," I said.

"You did great. We're at the top of the run where we skied before. Let's ski down it again."

And off we went for several more laps of the bunny hill. I fell a few times, and getting up was a challenge. I didn't know if my skis were parallel to the slope or pointed slightly downhill, so when I stood up, I could easily start moving before I was ready. Sometimes I couldn't tell if I was standing still or gliding very slowly, and I eventually learned to drag a pole to feel whether I was moving or not.

After several trips down, Muriel said, "I think you're ready for the real mountain. I'll guide you over to the main lift, and we can go over to West Buttermilk."

I remembered West Buttermilk from my college skiing. Mostly green runs. I called them cruisers. Gently rolling runs. But where the bunny hill was wide open, these runs were narrower and had trees on the sides. That thought added a little extra focus.

Immediately, I felt the slightly steeper pitch, which made me go faster. Because the runs were narrow, the turns came closer together. No super long traverses. I liked the feeling, but I needed to develop the confidence in this blind-skiing system and my guides to be comfortable that I could go faster and faster.

At the end of the day, Ginny was waiting at the base. "How did it go?" she asked.

"It was great. Muriel is a great teacher, and we progressed to being able to go up the lift."

"Bill's a great student," Muriel said. "It really helps that he had skied some when he could see."

"How was your lesson?" I asked Ginny.

"It was fine. There are seven or eight others in the class, so we have to wait on each other. I fell quite a few times, but I'm getting a little more comfortable with it."

Over the ensuing years, I learned that the components of skiing well included my confidence in the guide, the guide's confidence in me, his or her experience guiding, my skiing technique, and the snow conditions. As both the guide's confidence and mine grew and my technique improved, my speed increased, and I became comfortable on steeper terrain.

Muriel and I skied the rest of the day and every morning that week. She told me things that I'd heard before.

"Keep your weight forward. You should be balanced on your skis. Hands out front, like you're holding a lunch tray. Stand up tall and let the skis do the work."

She pointed out that I'd been holding a defensive posture with my weight toward the back, and I had a tendency to drop my hands. Everything about my form was wrong, but I learned to fight down the runs, and most importantly, it was a blast.

Skiing was really fun. I loved the speed and everything else about it. It felt like skiing used to, and I was delighted—especially since walking with a cane didn't feel like walking had before I was blinded. I could always hear my guide's voice, but my overall sense was that I was doing it all myself. The guide's commands seemed like my own thoughts.

The next morning at breakfast, the same man I'd talked to the first morning said, "I see you're still alive. The skiing must have gone well."

"Yes," I said. "I was pretty happy with my first day. My instructor was great, and the system of commands is simple. I just need to pay attention and follow directions."

"Where did you ski?" he asked.

"We stuck to West Buttermilk and one run to the bottom under the main lift."

"Good for you," he said. "Maybe we'll see you out there today."

I fell ten or twelve times a day that first week. The snow was uneven, and unseen bumps often jolted me off balance and I went down.

"Keep your knees bent," Muriel said. "They're your shock absorbers. You'll learn to absorb those bumps in your legs."

The runs on West Buttermilk were pretty easy, but several of them funneled into a pretty steep pitch close to the bottom.

"Just go slow, and you'll be OK," Muriel said.

As she called my first turn, I picked up a lot of speed. This was steep!

"Hold, hold," she said as I scraped off some of the speed. I remembered skiing this run sighted, and it wasn't that big of a deal. But today it felt very steep and long. Over the course of that week, I became more comfortable, but I continued to fall at least once every time we went down this pitch.

At the end of the day, Muriel said, "There's a shop right here where we can leave your skis, poles, and boots overnight. It's called Leave It at Leo's. They cater to newer skiers and are very helpful. I had someone from the rental shop take your street shoes over there this morning."

She left her skis and poles in a rack and showed me over to Leo's. We entered a warm room, and Muriel said, "Sit on this bench and loosen your boots. Someone will come over to help you in a minute.

"Hello Muriel," a man's voice said.

"Hi Leo," she responded. "I want you to meet Bill Johnson. Today was his first day to ski blind, and he did really well. He's planning to ski all week."

"Great. I'm Leo," he said. "Samantha, could you come over and help Mr. Johnson?" he called. He then turned back to me. "Sam will help you get your boots off, and we'll store all your equipment for you until tomorrow," he said.

"Hi Mr. Johnson, I'm Sam. Did you have fun today?" she asked.

"Yes. It was really great."

"Let me help you with those buckles," she said.

As she loosened the buckles, the feeling came back into my feet. They were all tingles and pinpricks. She lifted up my first boot and said, "Here, I'll just pull them off for you."

Wow. *What a service*, I thought. She then took all my equipment, came back with my street shoes, and went to help the next guest.

Leo sat down to chat a little as his employees hustled around. He liked to get to know his customers and was very friendly.

"Did Sam take good care of you, Bill?" he asked.

"Yes. All your people seem so pleasant and helpful. You must really run a tight ship," I said.

"We try," he answered. Then he leaned over and whispered like a conspirator in my ear. "She's one of the most attractive people I've ever hired. A real knockout. I just thought you'd like to know."

I laughed. "I'm not surprised. I picture all the people I meet as being attractive. Why would I want to picture them as anything else?" I asked.

As the time of my blindness increased, I remembered how the people I knew had looked the last time I saw them. But now there were so many new people in my life, and I needed to create a picture of what they looked like. The visions I created were based on their demeanor, voice, and who knows what else. I occasionally tested my picture of someone with a trusted friend and found out that the vision I created bore no relationship to how people really looked. Since the great majority of people are friendly and pleasant, I picture them in pretty undefined, but attractive, terms.

———▬———

My first week in Aspen I met Sid, Ann, Laura, and others. They were all experienced guides. While they each had a slightly different style of guiding, they used the same basic set of commands and techniques. As we rode the lifts, I had plenty of time to get to know each of them. They were all very personable people who volunteered their time to guide blind skiers. We all got along great, and I came to realize that I'd made many friends in Aspen.

Skiing gave me the feeling of freedom and independence that I'd lost seven months earlier, and I loved it. Peter, the director of the BOLD program, and I talked every evening about how that day had gone. He encouraged me to give feedback about the guides, and he sometimes had some suggestions from them for me. Then he'd tell me who I'd be skiing with the next day.

One of my guides was the publisher of *The Aspen Times*. He was in his seventies, and he scared me a little. He didn't seem as cautious as Muriel. At one point, we needed to cut over from West Buttermilk to Main, about mid-mountain.

"Here, I'll grab your pole," he said. "We have to get up some speed to make it, so just keep your skis parallel. Let's go."

And we pushed over a dropoff. We were quickly going faster than I had the previous days. Maybe twice as fast.

"Doing good. Just a little further," he said. "Now up a hill, and stop to your right. How did you like that?

"Better now that we're stopped," I said. "That was faster than I've gone. A little scary, but it was fun."

"We'll do it again, and you'll get used to it."

That first trip to Aspen was a break from the real world and, man, I really needed it. I was tired of people telling me that I'd be limited for the rest of my life. I simply didn't believe it. There were still many uncertainties, but skiing was a great confidence builder and a lot of fun. I got nothing but kudos and encouragement from everyone around me. To the people at the ski area and my guides, blind skiers weren't uncommon. I met Tina, Nancy, and Mario—all blind skiers—in Aspen.

I wore the orange bib back to the lodge after skiing. On many afternoons, Ginny and I went straight to Little Annie's for après-ski—happy hour. I often heard, "Was that you that I saw skiing at Buttermilk?"

"It was," I'd answer.

"You looked great. I don't think I could do that. That's amazing."

I got more positive encouragement everywhere I went. It felt fantastic. That trip was the reinvigoration and the shot in the arm that I needed. I'd found a recreational activity that I enjoyed immensely, and it was obviously something I could do. It also offered me the potential for future growth as a skier.

I hadn't yet gotten back to skiing Aspen Highlands, which had been my favorite mountain back in college. Not to mention Snowmass and Ajax. Snowmass had always been beyond my abilities, and Ajax, I hadn't dared to ski. It had the reputation of being almost all single- and double-black diamond runs. Definitely beyond my ability. But I knew I could get better.

That week I met a bunch of great people who treated me like they treated everyone else. While Ginny and others in my life back in Saint Louis seemed comfortable with me, other friends never quite relaxed. Maybe seeing me reminded them of what I'd lost. But I was focused on what I still had and could still gain. Skiing was at the top of that list, as was Ginny.

I was determined to get my life back and function in the world just as I had before. I would be professional and competent in the business world, but I had to learn how to put people at ease with me. I needed a strategy to reverse the preconceptions they had, to crush their low expectations about what I could do.

In Aspen, my guides were familiar enough with blindness to joke around with me. "I thought you saw that," they might say if I got hung up with one ski on each side of a lift line divider. Or, if my lunch looked better than their own, I'd hear, "I'm swapping lunches with you. You'll never know, right?" All in good humor, and it made me laugh at the funny situations I found myself in. I got comfortable sharing the humorous moments with those around me and learned it was an easy way to interact with others.

My sense of humor became my tool for putting others at ease, and I found that I enjoyed the self-deprecating type. Some people didn't always get it, but it was much healthier to be able to see humor in my new challenges rather than get overly frustrated and depressed about things that used to be simple. Having this perspective allowed me to step away from the frustrations, and my sense of humor overcame the temptation to fall into darker moods.

Ginny and I had a great week. It was our first Valentine's day together, and we had so much fun exploring what Aspen had to offer to us both. Vacations can sometimes be the end of relationships, but when we headed home, we were closer than ever.

CHAPTER
NINETEEN

"Now can we get a Seeing Eye Dog, Daddy?" Kelly had asked when she'd first seen me in the hospital.

"Good idea," was all I could say. Kelly had scrambled up on my hospital bed and didn't seemed at all concerned with my wounds, the bad haircut from the operation, or the couple of tubes that were still attached to me. Her focus had been on that tangible, lovable icon of blindness: The Seeing Eye Dog.

I'd always been a dog lover and had adopted a black lab-Irish setter mix in college. When she was killed by a delivery truck, my girlfriend and I cried as we carried her into a car and rushed her to the vet. She made it there, but her injuries were too much for her.

When I came back to Lawrence from Aspen, I brought my new dog, Canyon, with me, and she was my buddy through graduate school. When I graduated and moved back home, Mom and Dad welcomed her. Dad and I constructed a wire run for her in the back yard since their yard wasn't fenced.

My first job after college was as a dealer rep for Chrysler, and my travel schedule didn't allow me to keep a dog, so my parents kept Canyon for more than a year. When it became apparent that I wouldn't be able to take her back for quite some time, they found her a good home on a farm.

Canyon still had the excess of energy that Irish Setters and puppies are known for, and she could be a handful.

After my first blind ski trip, I started thinking about whether or not I wanted to get a guide dog, so I contacted several local guide dog users.

"Are you a dog lover?" was always their first question.

"Yes."

"Good. That's the first thing to consider when thinking about getting a guide dog. It's still a dog, and you have to care for and love your dog or it won't work out," one of the guide dog owners told me.

"Where do I get one?" I asked.

"There are many schools around the country. Two of the oldest and most respected are The Seeing Eye in Morristown New Jersey, and Guide Dogs for the Blind in San Rafael, California. The Lions club also trains dogs in Michigan, and there are others."

"Where did you get yours?" I asked.

"I went to The Seeing Eye. I think they're the best. They were the first in this country, and the name *Seeing Eye Dog* originated with this school. As other schools were started, the industry developed the generic term of guide dog, but Seeing Eye Dog still persists, kind of like Kleenex.

"Why should I get a guide dog if I'm happy with my cane?" I asked.

"Good question. I like my dog because we can walk faster than I do with my cane, and my dog has learned my normal routes and trips. I just follow. It's so easy."

It sounded like it could be a pretty good fit for me, so I decided to pursue the opportunity. Other discussions confirmed that The Seeing Eye and Guide Dogs for the Blind each had their following and supporters. I contacted them both.

"Have you had a guide dog before?" the admissions person at The Seeing Eye asked.

"No."

"How long have you been blind?"

"About seven months."

"Have you had orientation and mobility training?" came the next question.

"Yes, I went to Lions World in Little Rock."

Again, I learned that I was ahead of the prescribed schedule everyone thought I should follow. A reasonable requirement to get a guide dog would be to have well-developed orientation skills. And I did. But the *general* guideline was that a person needed at least a year from the time they were blinded to refine their orientation skills sufficiently before getting a guide dog.

"I do well with my cane and walk all around my neighborhood," I exaggerated slightly.

"Do you work?"

"I'm planning to go back to work in the next couple of months."

After some more discussion, The Seeing Eye representative said she would send me an application form to fill out.

"Is there someone who can help you fill it out?" she asked.

"Yes," I answered. I wondered if there were blind people who were so isolated that they didn't have anyone in their life to help them fill out a form. Another reminder to be grateful for everything I had.

"Good. One of our field support people will contact you to schedule a home visit. When our admissions department has your application and the report from the visit, they'll decide if you're a good candidate for a dog."

I immediately felt like I was applying for college again. Mom helped me fill out the application, and the field representative scheduled a visit for the following week.

"Hi Bill, I'm John, from The Seeing Eye," he said when I answered the door.

He confirmed the information in my application about my living situation, how long I'd lived here, etc. Then he said, "Let's go for a Juneau walk."

"What's that?"

"It's a way for me to gather some information that will help us match you to a dog," he said. "I have a harness that I'll hold low, as if it were on a dog. You grab it with your left hand and follow where it goes. I'll stop at down curbs and pause at up curbs, just like our dogs. When we come to an intersection, I'll stop and then you tell me whether to go straight, left, or right. Of course, if we're crossing a street, you should decide when we can safely cross. Here, feel this harness."

"Wow, it's leather," I said.

"This rigid part is the handle that you hold with your left hand. Are you ready to go?"

"Yes."

We went outside to the street in front of my house. "Hold this handle," he said. "I'll pull you just like a dog would."

And off we went, heading up that same block where I had learned about pickup truck mirrors eight months earlier. Walking at a brisk pace, I felt a little uncomfortable without my cane. I'd learned to trust my cane technique to keep me from walking directly into something. Walking with both hands at my side was a bit unnerving.

"Is this too fast?" he asked.

"No. You could go a little faster. This is fun," I said through a grin.

When we got to the corner, the handle stopped. It was the same corner that I'd been afraid to cross before I had my cane.

"Which way should we go to get in a few more blocks before we go back to your house?"

"Turn right."

When we crossed the street, the handle paused slightly, and he said, "We're coming to a curb. Your dog will slow to get your attention, and you should say 'hup' to get up the curb."

"Hup," I said and followed the handle down the sidewalk to the next corner where it stopped.

"Which direction should we go?" he asked.

"Turn left," I said.

"Say *left* as you pull back on the handle, and point your right hand to the left. That's how we train this move. The dog will back up a bit to give you room to turn."

"Left," I said as I pulled back. "That felt neat," I said as the handle did a smooth maneuver, and I followed it across the street to our left.

As the handle paused at the next up curb, I said "Hup." Around the block we went, then back home. He walked pretty quickly, but I kept up well.

"What did you think?" he asked

"That was great," I said. "We walked faster than I normally do with my cane, but it felt good. Kind of fun."

"I'll write up my report, and you should hear something from the school within a few days."

Now the waiting started. Never in my wildest dreams had I imagined I'd be sweating out whether I'd be accepted to the guide dog school of my choice. I hadn't had a dog since Canyon, and I really liked the idea. Business travel wouldn't be a hindrance to dog ownership anymore because my dog would travel with me.

Toward the end of that week, I was accepted by The Seeing Eye school, and I scheduled my month of training for April 1992. I'd planned to go back to work around March first, so I'd get a month of work under my belt, then leave for a month to get my Seeing Eye Dog. It seemed like a good way to ease back into work.

———■———

I was back on the payroll in early March, and I talked to my new boss in Chicago, Neil. I knew Neil, and he was a good guy. I was happy to get away from Ken.

"You know you'll have the same objectives as all of the other Senior Managers, don't you?" Neil said.

"That's what I want," I said. "I know that client billing is what pays the rent, not to mention my salary, and I want to carry my own weight. Maybe it won't work out, but I have to give it a shot."

"It will be a learning experience for both of us," Neil said.

"Agreed, and thanks for your and the firm's willingness to let me give it a shot. I wouldn't be comfortable if I didn't try."

Our firm, which was primarily an accounting firm, assigned administrative assistants to work with two or three partners at a time. And those partners' practice teams used that same admin person.

"We expect you may need extra admin support with reading and other things," Neil said, "so for purposes of admin support, you'll be treated as a partner. That should give you the support you need."

"Thanks," I said. "That's very generous and sounds great."

"As you get back into the job, if there are any problems at all, just let me know," Neil said. With that, I was back to work.

Having already explored our office building a bit, I was comfortable with the logistics of getting to work that first day. All I needed was a taxi cab and my trusty white cane. This was what I'd been aiming for during the last seven months, and now it was time to make things happen. I had learned the skills I needed to do the job; the challenge now was to use those skills.

I didn't know how clients, especially new ones, would accept a blind management consultant. We consultants loved to write on white boards as we talk with our clients, and I couldn't do that anymore, So, how would they react? Would they trust my advice? These questions could only be answered by giving it my best shot. I didn't want to ever look back and think, *What if?*

My boss was in Chicago, but Vince Cannella, the Saint Louis office managing partner, called the shots in the local office. He thought I should sit close to Kristine, my administrative assistant, and suggested I move into Tony Lake's old office because she sat right outside the door. That office was larger than mine and had a couple of side chairs in addition to the two chairs in front of the desk. Vince thought the extra room would be helpful when I came back with my Seeing Eye Dog.

That was all very thoughtful, but moving into Tony's office struck me as odd. I also thought it would have been even more so for others, but I kept my thoughts to myself. I occupied that office for over a year until we moved to a different floor. I was glad to be out of it. It would always be Tony's office, and it was a sad reminder to everyone who met with me there.

During that first month, many of my coworkers from different practices dropped in to say hi and offered their condolences about the events of July 2. Their heartfelt expressions of sorrow for Tony and support for me meant a lot. We all needed to get this behind us and go forward.

Now it was time to establish a routine with Kristine. Every day, she read the mail to me. We decided how she could format the letters and reports that I planned to create on my new MS DOS PC, complete with Word Perfect. No more yellow pads for me.

Linda, who had helped me with the presentation in Atlanta, was also instrumental in my return. She and I spent time together to review her existing projects, and she told me where all the rest of Tony's team had ended up. Just seven months later, only Linda, me, and one other person from the old group were left, and that other person left as soon as I returned. Linda had kept herself somewhat chargeable with a variety of projects, but they weren't substantial, and there were no short-term projects in the Network and Telecom area that we'd come from. We were starting from scratch. Our challenge was to sell some work.

That first month went by quickly. I made calls to many of the fellow employees with whom I'd worked over the years to let them know that I was back at work and in need of some chargeable work. They all knew our practice area and promised to keep their eyes open for telecom opportunities. I also touched base with several past clients and a couple of vendor contacts. Everyone wanted to hear how I was doing, and they agreed to keep their ear to the ground for opportunities where I could provide value.

I'd done well in getting reestablished. But I hadn't uncovered a good sales opportunity, or better yet, a "blue bird." That's what we called work that just appeared out of the blue. Of course, opportunities almost never come from nowhere. But with past clients of my own—and sometimes the firm's—the normal sales cycle is shortened because of the prior relationships. I hoped that the contacts I'd made would amount to something by the time I got back with my Seeing Eye Dog.

———▬———

New dog users spent four weeks at The Seeing Eye school to be matched with a dog; to be trained in how to keep the dog's skills sharp; and to learn how to care for the dog's needs. They were actually training the new handler, not the dog. The dogs were already perfectly trained when the prospective new handlers showed up.

The material I got from The Seeing Eye listed what to bring with me for that month. Other than a normal mix of clothing and personal items, they said to bring rain gear. Thinking nothing of it, I packed my umbrella.

A Seeing Eye employee met me at the airport gate. He helped me get my luggage, and we met up with other arriving students for the ride back to Morristown. When I arrived at The Seeing Eye campus, someone immediately noticed my umbrella.

"Let me take your umbrella," the woman said.

"What if it rains?" I asked.

"We'll help you get some rain gear. It's kind of dangerous to other people and their eyes for you to use an umbrella," she said, placing my hand on the nubs at the outer edge of the umbrella.

"I never thought about that, but I understand," I said sheepishly. There were still more dos and don'ts for me to learn about being a blind person.

I was shown the way to my room, the TV lounge on our floor, and the dining room. Since all rooms had a private bath, I had everything I needed.

Other students arrived, and we enjoyed getting to know each other. There were about twelve of us who would start this session together. Some of them were back for a second, third, or fourth dog, but there were also several who were here for their first dog like me.

I got familiar with my room. There were two beds, although I didn't have a roommate, nightstands by each bed, a closet, and two dressers by the bathroom door. I unpacked my suitcase and put all my stuff in the dresser. Shaving kit in the bathroom, radio next to the bed.

Then I lay down on my bed. Here I was again, off on a new adventure—like when I came home from the hospital and when I went to Little Rock. I was all alone with a new challenge. Would a Seeing Eye dog be a good fit for me and help me live a full life? I didn't know for sure, but I was going to give it my best effort. The special relationship between a blind person and their Seeing Eye dog was the stuff of legend. I was ready to have that very special experience.

———————

"Mr. Johnson?" a man's voice asked.

"Bill Johnson," I replied.

"I'm Walt Sutton. I'll be your trainer during your time here. Can we talk?"

"Sure."

"I have your application here. Just let me confirm a few things. You were blinded last July by a gun shot?"

"Yes. It was a random shooting in Atlanta."

"That's terrible. Can you see anything at all?" he asked.

"No. Just a little light perception, but it doesn't help me get around. You should consider me a total."

"OK. And you've been through orientation and mobility training?" he asked.

"Yes, for three months at the Lions World School for the Blind in Little Rock, Arkansas."

"That's interesting. There's a woman coming in today who's from Little Rock. She's getting her second or third dog. Did you like the O&M training?

"I loved it. After I finished some of the other daily living classes, I scheduled all my time with O&M. At the end, I was doing over three hours a day."

"You look to be in pretty good shape. You aren't diabetic, right?"

"Not diabetic. I don't know how good of shape I'm in. I did a lot of walking in Arkansas, and went skiing for a week last month, but I don't know about being in shape."

"What? You went skiing? How'd you do?" he asked.

"It was a blast, and I think I skied OK."

"It says in the notes that you're open to any breed for your dog. Is that right?"

"I'd love a Labrador, but I'll trust you to make the best match for me. I've never been close to any German Shepherds, but I know many people love them. I trust your judgement."

"OK. I've got some others to talk to. You're free until dinner. We start tomorrow with your training," he said.

"When do I get my dog?" I asked.

"Tomorrow. We'll give you some instructions and get more familiar with your requirements before we match you with a dog."

I could tell there was a definite difference between those who'd come back for a replacement dog and those of us who were first timers. The experienced ones knew the routine and the ropes, and they helped me get oriented to the building and grounds. Some of them were such hard-core guide dog users that they didn't use a cane at all. I'd become pretty fond of my cane and wondered if I'd give it up completely when I got my dog.

The women were housed on a connecting wing, and we shared a TV room and lounge. We were a diverse group from all over the country. The group included a retired judge, a woman who was about to be married, a man who'd taught martial arts before being shot and blinded, a piano tuner, and a woman who worked in an air traffic control in California. In general, they were older and better established in life than the group at Lions World. I felt right at home.

When dinner was announced, we all made our way down the stairs to the dining room. That first night's meal was great, and they had very good desserts. We were served by very pleasant employees, just like in a restaurant. This was so different from the cafeteria at Lions World.

After breakfast the next morning, Walt showed up at my door. "Are you ready to get started?"

"Yes," I answered, full of nervous anticipation.

"First we'll take a Juneau walk. I want to confirm the notes from your home visit regarding your strength and pace when you walk. You can leave your cane here. I'll give you an elbow until we get outside.

Outside, Walt positioned the harness handle.

"Why do you call it a Juneau walk? Was there a dog named Juneau?" I asked.

"In Greek mythology," he answered, "Juneau was Jupiter's wife. The ancient Greeks prayed to Juneau for a good match in marriage. We want to make a good match between the handler and his or her dog, which in some ways is even more intimate than a marriage.

"Here take this. This harness has a leash in addition to the handle. Feel it?"

"Got it," I said.

"The leash is attached to the harness at both ends, so it forms a big loop. Put your hand at the end of it, and wrap the leash around your wrist. Then grab the handle."

We took off at a moderate pace, but Walt sped up considerably. "Is this pace comfortable?"

"Yes, " I answered. We continued around the grounds of The Seeing Eye. He gave a quick tug on the handle a couple of times, but I didn't lose my grip.

"Good. If you ever lose the handle, just stop. You still have the dog on the leash, so he's not going anywhere. Just find the handle again and say hup or forward."

We walked for some time with Walt speeding up and slowing down as we covered different terrain.

Back in my room, I had some free time while Walt worked with others in our group. Ron, who had the room across the hall from me, was also here for his first dog.

I'd learned in Little Rock that most blind people ask each other, "How long have you been blind? How did it happen?" And, "Can you see anything?" No two people's blindness is exactly the same, and most enjoy explaining the little bits of vision they still have. There's a continuum of partial vision due to diabetes, Retinitis Pigmentosa, and macular degeneration. Not to mention gunshot wounds.

"How long have you been blind?" I asked Ron when I found out he was here for his first dog.

"About a year."

"How did it happen?" I asked.

"I was shot by a burglar, but I don't like talking about it."

"I was shot too." I said. "I don't mind talking about it if you ever want to."

"OK," he answered

I came to know Ron as a nice, but subdued, man. I later learned that Ron had known the burglar and was quite bitter about having been blinded. Apparently, he focused his negative energy and anger on the burglar.

Was Ron's angry, unhappy reaction what everyone had expected from me? Why was I given the gift of almost immediate acceptance of what had happened, when others weren't? I didn't know the answers, and since I'd never seen my attacker, I really hadn't experienced the violence. I had no face to focus on. I knew that a person had shot me for no reason, but emotionally, I didn't feel like I'd experienced violence. My blinding seemed like a random event—wrong place at the wrong time. Yes, I knew there was a person who held the gun and pulled the trigger, but I couldn't work up any anger toward him for my situation. For the killing of Tony and Keith? Yes! But not for me.

That night as I went to bed, I was grateful that I'd accepted my blindness and that I could talk about what happened on July 2, 1991—and my life today—without undue emotion. I almost felt like that day's events had happened to someone else. I thought that living without acceptance would be very difficult, and I was grateful for my experience.

Walt found me after lunch to learn more about my lifestyle, so he could make a good match for me.

"What's your neighborhood like? Do you have sidewalks?" he asked.

"Some streets have sidewalks, some not."

"Do you travel on business? On airplanes?"

"Yes," I said. "I'm just returning to work, but in the past I traveled several days a week to visit clients all over the country."

"Did you know you can take your dog on the plane?" Walt asked.

"Yes. Where do they sit?"

"We'll instruct you in that later, but for now I'll tell you that they stay at your feet, under the seat in front of you."

I was given a lot of supplies that I'd need to care for my dog: two large metal bowls, an eighteen-inch bed chain, a grooming comb and brush, and a Kong Ball dog toy. I also got a harness and some saddle soap.

"The harness is new and is still pretty stiff," Walt said. "Your dog will love it if you soften it up a bit with the saddle soap. Just rub it in with the cloth, and really work the leather straps. Don't worry about the handle—just the straps that go around the dog's chest, front, and underbelly.

You'll be introduced to your dog after dinner."

———◼———

It was finally time. Walt came to my room to get me.

"Leave that cane here. You won't be needing it anymore," he said as he offered me an elbow. "You can sit in the lounge while I get your dog. I'll be right back."

I sat in the lounge and waited. I had been looking forward to this moment for months. I was both nervous and giddy with the prospect of meeting my new buddy. Ten months ago, a Seeing Eye dog was the furthest thing from my thoughts. Now I was excited to meet my new partner.

"Heel," I heard Walt say as he approached. He came closer and sat down.

"Sit on the floor, Bill. I've got your dog. His name is Darby. When you're ready, clap your hands and call him. He'll come right over to you."

I got on my knees and clapped my hands. "Come Darby," I said.

I heard his paws on the floor as I clapped again. Then he was on me. He licked my face as I petted and felt him all over. "Good boy. Good Darby," I said as he settled down a little. I rubbed his back and felt his head and ears.

"He feels like a Labrador," I said.

"He's a black male Labrador retriever," Walt said.

"Oh, Darby. You're beautiful," I said. Darby was very solid with a much boxier head than my old setter/lab mix female.

"Sixty-two pounds." Walt said. "And that's a good weight for him. He's very healthy. We bred him here."

"I said I didn't care which breed I got, but I really wanted a Labrador," I said.

""I could tell," Walt said. "But Darby was already the dog I've had in mind for you for a couple of weeks. The last two days confirmed that you two are a good team."

Team, I thought. Wow.

"Let me show you two back to your room. You can play with the Kong Ball and get to know each other."

Darby had lots of energy and seemed like he already knew what a Kong Ball was. When I tossed it across the room, it bounced unpredictably. I could hear Darby scramble on the slick floor to gain some traction, then to stop as he pounced on the ball. He always brought it back to me to throw again. He lived up to his name as a retriever. He always got a hug and a pat on the head when he brought it back.

Whenever I said, "Drop it," he always released the Kong ball. Would he never get tired of this game?

The door opened and Walt asked, "How are you guys doing?"

"Great," I answered. "He likes to play ball."

"It's time to water him and take him outside. Fill up the water bowl and put it on the floor for him. Let's take a look at your bed chain while he drinks," Walt suggested. "We recommend that he be on this chain every night."

"OK," I said as I filled the water bowl.

"The bed chain goes around the leg of the bed at the headboard end."

"It seems awfully short. Are you sure he'll be comfortable?" I asked.

"Yes. He's already familiar with a bed chain."

"I don't have a roommate. Can't I just keep the door closed and give him some room?"

"No," Walt answered. "If you keep him restrained and close to you, it speeds up the bonding process. I've been his master for the last several months, and we need him to understand that you are his master now."

As we talked, I could hear Darby. *Slurp, slurp, slurp.* Our play time had made him thirsty.

When he finished Walt said, "Now dump out the rest of the water and put the leash on him." As I dumped out the water, Walt continued. "You'll always keep your dog in your left hand, so if you take my left elbow, I'll show you down to the park where he can do his business."

I put on Darby's leash and wrapped it around my wrist as I'd been taught. I found Walt's elbow and said, "OK. Let's go."

"I'll show you the way tonight. Tomorrow morning, you'll feed and water Darby around 6:30. Someone will announce 'park time' shortly thereafter, and you'll have to find your way out here with your cane."

The "park" wasn't a park at all, but an asphalt pad they could hose down to keep everything sanitary.

"Move the clip on one end of your leash to the ring close to the other end," Walt instructed. "That will make your leash longer. Then try to keep Darby moving around you in a circle. He'll stop when he needs to do something." Tonight, Darby only needed to urinate.

"Tomorrow morning, he'll need to defecate, and you'll need to learn how to clean up after him."

Yikes. How would that work? I couldn't even see where he pooped. How would I know when he did it?

Walt showed us back to the room. I gave Darby a hug and a pat on the head, then clipped him to the bed chain. I pictured him looking at me sadly, but he didn't really seem to mind the bed chain. I was still excited about meeting my new buddy. I reached down to feel him several times through the night. Darby probably slept much more soundly than I did.

The next morning, I woke up early. I pushed the button on my talking watch which announced, "five thirty." As I lay in bed, I wondered what this day would bring. Just the logistics of getting the day going were daunting. I had to feed and water Darby, then get him out to the park, and clean up his poop?! Should I take a shower now or after we went outside? What time was breakfast again?

I reached down to pet Darby. How could this big dog curl up at the end of an eighteen-inch chain in the corner by the bed and the wall? He didn't seem to have a care, so I decided to get my shower out of the way while I had a chance.

Rather than having us all keep dog food in our rooms, they handed out a portion for every meal. When I heard the commotion in the hall, I opened my door and offered my food bowl. *Krisch, kirsch.* I heard the two scoops of food hit the bowl. Back inside, I put a little warm water on the food and filled Darby's water bowl. Then I let him off the bed chain.

Like any other Lab, he knew exactly what to do and wolfed down his food. Then he took a long drink of water while I got dressed for the New Jersey spring weather. I put his leash on and ventured into the hallway with my cane. Dog on the left, cane in the right hand. There were others heading to the same place, so I followed the crowd out to the park. One of the other trainers was there to instruct us in how to clean up after our dogs.

"You'll find small plastic bags in this dispenser by the door," he said, as he banged on it. "Grab one as you go outside. Everyone find a spot that isn't too close to anyone else. You want your dogs to do their business, not play with each other. You'll have to talk to each other to figure out your spacing."

"Hello. Who's there?" I heard.

"It's Bill. I'll move over a little. Anyone else over here?" Silence. Good.

"Let your leashes out and keep the dogs moving around you in a circle. When they stop, you need to walk up to them from the side and determine whether they're peeing or pooping."

"How do we do that?" someone asked.

"You feel the dogs back. Run your hand from his front shoulders towards his tail. If his back is arched, he's pooping. Then you put your foot back by his hind quarters, pointed toward where his mess will be. When he finishes, he'll walk away. Then take the bag you picked up and turn it inside out over your hand. Reach down and pick up the mess. With your leash hand, fold the bag back over the mess. You should then be able to tie the bag in a knot, or you can use a twist tie. If you've done a good job, there should be no mess, and you can put the bag in your pocket until you find a trash can."

Well, I thought, that's how that works. It wasn't as difficult or dangerous as I'd feared. It soon became second nature.

Breakfast with the dogs was interesting. We were challenged to keep our dog under our own chair. By pulling the leash taut and sticking it under my thigh, I could theoretically tell if Darby was moving. I pictured the scene under the table. Six people in chairs with six dogs on the floor, eyeing each other in their own little world. The dogs were mostly quiet. I was impressed; they were trained so well.

After breakfast, Walt said, "We're going for a walk. I'll show each of you how to put on your dog's harness and how tight to make it. Bill, let's do yours first. Hold the harness by this back strap, and hold the straps that buckle together under your palm."

"Like this?" I asked.

"Good. Now put the chest strap over the dog's nose and place the harness on his back. Now buckle the harness. Reach the leather end under the dog and thread it through the loop in the front strap and into the buckle on the other side. Put it on the second hole, and let me feel how tight it is."

Walt grabbed the buckle strap and slid his hand behind it. "The second hole is the right one for Darby. Remember that. Pretty soon, it'll be worn into the leather."

He got everyone set up and said, "Follow me outside. Your dog should stop at the top of the stairs. When he does, wave your right hand in front of you and say forward."

"Good dog, Darby," I said as several teams followed Walt. Then, "Let's go."

Darby got up, and I followed him across the room to the stairs. Would he stop? Would I fall down the stairs? I thought as my steps became tentative.

Darby stopped. I felt in front of me with my toe and found the stair. Amazing. "Good dog," I said as I patted his neck. "Forward," I said, and we went down the stairs. I trusted him at the top of the stairs and he didn't fail me. This was a great start.

Outside, Walt said, "There's a paved path around the campus where you can walk whenever you want. It's called the Leisure Path. For those of you who are getting your first dog, my advice is to follow your dog."

"What does that mean?" someone asked.

"It means you don't try to steer him with the handle. Also, don't push him or hold him back too much. You'll get the hang of it, but at first, just keep a firm grip and follow your dog."

"Forward," I said firmly as I pointed ahead with my right hand. Darby took off down the paved walkway. The handle felt solid in my hand. Darby seemed to know what to do. On we walked; there were no decisions to make. Just follow my dog. He moved at a good pace, not too fast, and definitely not too slow. I thought I moved pretty well with a cane when I was comfortable with my route, but Darby would prove to be faster.

We passed another student or two, and eventually got back to Walt.

"How did it go?" he asked.

"It was great. He's on a mission. Just walking."

"I was Darby's trainer, " Walt said. "He was always a very willing dog. I think you two will do well."

The next day, we loaded up two or three teams in a van and went to downtown Morristown. There were lessons about transportation also.

"Always have your dog ride on the floor of a vehicle. If there's an accident, that's the safest place for them. Also, always reach behind the dog to make sure his tail isn't in the door before you close it. It happens that doors get slammed on tails, but you really don't want to be around that, and you definitely don't want it to happen to your dog."

I would never have thought of that.

"When we get to town," Walt continued, "I'll follow each of you individually around the block and across the street a couple of times. By this afternoon, we'll be able to walk in a pack, but I want to teach you each a few things individually first."

When it was my turn, Walt said, "Go ahead and take off. I'll be behind you all the way. When we get to the next intersection, Darby will walk up to the curb and stop. Feel in front of you with your toe, and if you don't feel the curb, say hup hup, and he'll move slowly forward until you feel it. Then praise him."

"Forward," I said, and we took off. We walked straight down the sidewalk until Darby stopped. I felt with my right toe, and the curb was right there. "Good boy, Darby. Good boy." I said as I scratched the top of his head.

"Which way can you turn without crossing a street?" Walt asked.

"Left."

"Good. Turn Left," he confirmed.

"Left," I said as I waved my right hand to the left. Darby backed up a bit to clear a path for me to turn left, and paused at the down curb. "Foreward," I said, and promptly followed him into the street. Just like on my first Juneau walk in Saint Louis. We walked around a couple of blocks with Walt occasionally testing my orientation with questions like, "Where is the traffic?" and, "Which way is the van?"

By afternoon, Walt trusted we were safe enough for a couple of teams to walk together with him following behind. One team went first, the next followed, and Walt brought up the rear.

We did a lot of walking and a lot of learning. I learned how to keep Darby's attention on his work. If we passed a yard with a barking dog, I could feel his head turn toward it.

"Hup, hup," I would say. "Good boy Darby. Good boy." I could feel his pace pick up, and he was back on the job.

There was no question that Darby was well trained, but I needed to learn how to maintain that training—and he needed to know I was his master. Walt taught me an obedience routine to practice with him daily. He also said that Darby was trained to pick up things that I might drop. I threw a set of keys a few feet away, and said, "Find the keys. Find the keys." More often than not, Darby would point to them with his nose, but that was a skill I didn't reinforce over time.

Thankfully, the staff taught us about veterinary care.

"Many vets provide free, or reduced-price care for service dogs," the instructor said. "If you can't afford the care your dog needs, let us know. The Seeing Eye has a foundation that can help. We want our dogs to be healthy, so they can provide good service to you."

Then she taught us how to keep our dogs' ears clean by using cotton balls and hydrogen peroxide. I learned that Labs, in particular, have lots of ear problems if their ears aren't kept clean. Next came the overall grooming.

"We want your dogs to always look their best. It reflects well on you, and on The Seeing Eye. You have two different grooming aids: a metal-toothed comb and a slicker brush. Use the comb first. This will clean out their undercoat, especially for the Labs. You should comb out a fair amount of hair every time you groom your dog, depending on the season. Then follow up with the slicker brush to clean up any loose fur. Do that three days a week, and your dog should always look his best."

We went downstairs to the grooming area to give it a try.

"Here's your grooming bench," my trainer said, slapping it. "Get Darby to jump up here."

I guided Darby to the bench and said, "Hup up." He jumped right up on the bench.

"Now use the comb," she instructed.

The metal comb got traction in Darby's thick lab coat. "Wow, this is a lot of fur," I said. "Where should I put it?"

"That's not too much," she said. "You can put it in the trash can over here," she said as she banged on it.

It felt good to remove so much hair. I pictured it making him cooler as the weather warmed.

———■———

We practiced crossing streets with and without traffic signals and with and without stop signs. I relied on my own orientation to decide when to cross. Darby's role was to be my fail safe. He was trained to always pay attention.

"If you make an unsafe decision, he should refuse to go," Walt said. "So never try to push or pull your dog when he doesn't want to go. Coax him with the forward command all you want, but if he won't move, don't make him. You'll learn to sense his reactions as you two work together. We call this intelligent disobedience, and it's something that differentiates our training from other schools."

We had something of an obstacle course to navigate— various scenarios that were controlled but required our dogs to make quick decisions. In one such exercise, Darby backed up when we were a couple of steps into an alley as a car driven by an instructor unexpectedly pulled in front of us. Darby had it under control. The only question was whether I could grasp the situation, feel his cue, and then back up with him. I was the one in training.

Our daily walks included recognizing low hanging branches, finding sections of sidewalk under construction, and other obstacles. The dogs were trained to stop when they approach a branch that is at head height or lower. Darby was very good at stopping, but of course, I wouldn't know why he stopped. If I sensed that we weren't close to a cross street, I felt for a curb or obstruction with my toe. If I didn't find anything, I reached out in front of me with my right hand. If I felt a branch, I'd say, "Good boy. Right," and we'd walk to the curb. It was the same for sidewalk repairs or any obstacle that Darby didn't want to negotiate. If he bumped me into a sign post or other obstacle, I dropped his harness and slapped the offending sign post and said, "Bad, bad." That reminded Darby of how much room the two of us required together.

One day I was talking with the woman who worked in air traffic control in California. It sounded like an unusual place for a blind person to work, but I let it go.

"How are you liking your first dog?" she asked.

"He's fantastic. I think I'm going to like having him."

"You want to know another benefit of having a Seeing Eye dog?" she said. "You'll find that he's a chick magnet."

"Oh," I said, thinking about Ginny. I wasn't sure that was what I really needed. But it was rather amusing.

We went out with our dogs every day, morning and afternoon, to get more experience and be exposed to other different situations. It was usually two or three teams together with Walt. Toward the end of the month, we learned that our final confidence-building exercise was a trip to the garment district in New York City. If we could negotiate those crowds, we could trust our dogs in any situation.

It was late morning when we got to New York, and I'd never experienced sidewalks that busy.

"This is the garment district," Walt said. "There are merchants pulling racks of clothing down the sidewalks and crowds of people going every which way. At the intersections, there will be an army coming at you from across the street. All you have to do is trust your dog. He'll get you through."

I said, "Forward," and we took off down the sidewalk. It was amazing. "Good boy, Darby," I said. I could tell the sidewalk was packed, but Darby moved at a reasonable pace. He moved a bit right, then left, and I followed. He was like a running back looking for an opening in the defense. We came to a corner, and he stopped.

"Good boy," I praised him, while I scratched his head. I'd brought along a handful of dry dog food and gave him a couple of pieces for encouragement.

In addition to all the people sounds, we were bombarded with revving car engines, honking horns, and squealing brakes. Could it be any more chaotic? Darby stood at my side and waited patiently. When the mass of people surged forward, I said "Forward." And we took off.

I could tell that others passed us coming the other direction. Darby stopped at the up curb and waited for me to say, "hup-up." I did, and we went several more blocks like that. All without incident.

My heart pounded. I'd never visited this part of New York City, but from the cacophony of noise, I pictured our safe passage seeming impossible. But Darby had done it. I'd been jostled a little, but we had largely avoided the whole throng of people. Crossing the busy streets seemed like the easy part.

"How did you like that?" Walt's voice interrupted.

"Unreal," I said. "He did great. Is that as busy as it sounds like?"

"Maybe busier. You both did great. You're going to do fine at home."

A couple of days later, it was time to go home. My month at The Seeing Eye had passed quickly. I was confident that my friend, Darby, would help me regain my personal life and my work life. We were now a team.

Now my focus was on flying home with Darby. As the day got closer, I pictured the Saint Louis airport and wondered at which gate we would arrive. I knew that airport like the back of my hand, and I pictured Darby and me making it all the way to a taxi without having to call the Meet and Assist team. This just might work, I thought.

On the airplane, the flight attendants fussed over both of us. They seated me in a bulkhead, which I later learned, didn't offer the most floor space. I'd been taught how to push Darby, tail first under the seat in front of me, where he fit really well. There's more room than it appears, and except for needing to keep his tail away from the drink cart, it was a safe place for him.

But on this trip, he sprawled out on the floor between me and the bulkhead. The other two seats were empty, so it worked out.

"Can we pet him?" the flight attendants asked.

"Thanks for asking. Let me take his harness off. You can pet him when he's off duty."

They fussed over Darby and brought him a bowl of water. "Can he have any other snacks?" they asked.

"No thanks. He's happy with water."

"He's really handsome," one flight attendant said.

"Thanks. I just met him a month ago," I said. "We're a new team together, and this is our first flight."

"Let me know if there is anything I can do to make it easier for either of you."

"Thanks," I said, thinking that Darby really was a chick magnet. Getting that extra attention from the flight attendants was a nice bonus.

CHAPTER
TWENTY

After that first ski trip, I couldn't wait to get back to Aspen. I wanted to feel that freedom again and to stretch myself mentally and physically. With the ski lessons and my experiences with capable guides, I'd become a better skier. And as I became more comfortable with my abilities and the guide-skier partnership, I started to ski faster on Buttermilk's green and blue runs. It was thrilling, and I wanted more.

So, Ginny and I went back to Aspen the first chance I got eleven months later, for the first of three ski trips that year.

I arranged the trip with Peter from BOLD. On my second week, he said I'd be skiing with a different guide named David. I waited at Buttermilk for him when I heard a voice say, "Are you Bill?"

"Yes."

"I'm David. Where are your skis?"

"They're the K2's right over here."

"Let's grab them and get out of here."

"Where are we going?" I asked.

"I heard you know what you're doing, so we're going to Snowmass, a real ski mountain. I don't guide on Buttermilk. I let the other guides do that. I only guide where you can actually ski. Are you OK with that?"

"I'm game, if you think I can do it."

"From what Muriel told me, you'll be fine," he said.

It was about a fifteen-minute drive to get there. That day went fine, and I was pleased that I'd enlarged my skiing world to include Snowmass. The runs were longer and more difficult, and the connections between runs were more of a challenge. To keep from having to pole too much—which meant using the strength of my shoulders and arms with the poles to keep myself moving forward—we had to keep up our speed when we came off many of the runs in order to get all the way to the next run. It's no fun to have to pole, and it always wore me out.

David said, "After the next left turn, point your skis straight down the hill, and I'll come up on your left and grab your pole."

I always felt a little lost skiing "down the hill" as David put it. When I'm on a left or right turn, I have an edge of my ski in the snow, which felt more stable. Simply pointing my skis down the hill felt out of control.

"Now put your skis together and let's boogie," David said as he grabbed my pole and pulled me forward with him.

"On your left!" David hollered to some other skiers as we moved a little to the left.

"We're skiing down a service road," he told me, "and we're passing a bunch of slow skiers." I immediately pictured the skinny roads that meander up the ski slopes, which are used for support vehicles that service the ski resort. They're generally less than twenty feet wide, so skiers that move at different speeds are at risk of colliding.

"On your right!" he warned again.

"Now, I'll let you go, Bill. Make a left turn to a stop. Nicely done. We're at the top of the next run, and we got here without poling," David said.

David and I continued to ski a couple of days together every trip I took to Aspen. One day, he decided to take me to an area called the Big Burn near the top of Snowmass. A forest fire had burned off all of the trees many years before and they hadn't been replanted—hence the name Big Burn. It was a large, wide-open area with several runs defined for skiing. Often very windy and cold because there were no trees to break the wind, it provided a more advanced environment for me.

There were several runs that David wanted to try. One was a pretty long run, not terribly steep, but it was sometimes a little bumped up. Skiing moguls is the most difficult thing for me, and today it was peppered with what struck me as large moguls. It was mid-afternoon, and I was already tired, but there was no other way down.

"Keep your skis mostly downhill and try to feel the valleys. You want to stay in the valleys, instead of skiing over the top of the moguls." David said. "You'll have to feel where to turn. I'll try to call some turns when I can, but you'll be mostly on your own. It's wide open, and I'm not going anywhere."

"OK. How far does it go with moguls?" I asked.

"Probably one hundred yards. Push off straight ahead. Your first turn is a left—now!"

I felt my way through five or six turns before getting pointed too much toward the side. I launched myself off a big mogul and wiped out.

"That's hard work," I said.

"You looked good until that last one," David said.

I put my skis back on and took off. I repeated the launching experience several times. As I made my way down, all the accumulated strain from that morning's runs took its toll on my legs. They were burning. Eventually, we made it off the mogul run.

When we stopped, David asked, "How are you doing?"

"I'm whipped. That wasn't much fun."

"We'll take it easy getting to the bottom," he said.

For better or worse, my skiing experience had expanded that day, and I slept like a puppy that night.

David and I started skiing together a couple of days a week whenever I went back to Aspen—about three times a year. Ginny came with me once or twice each year, although she didn't keep up her own skiing. Aspen became a special place for us. It was a charming town with great restaurants and many great people. Fried clams and Fat Tire beer at Little Annie's after skiing remained a favorite. Fine dining at Pinion's with a stop at the bar afterward for a fine vintage port. We chose Taka Sushi for great sushi, and always ordered the squid salad.

On one trip, David said, "I'll pick you up at the Mountain House tomorrow, and we'll ski Ajax."

"You think I can do that?"

"I know that mountain better than Snowmass, and there's a lot of it you can ski. Plus, I like getting blind skiers out there. They don't see many of them."

The base area was right in town, so we could walk to the gondola. Getting on the gondola was another trick I had to learn.

From the top of Ajax, there's a route down to the base of the gondola that goes from Copper Gulch, to Spar, then Little Nell. They're all marked blue, but they'd actually be black at many other ski areas. Reasonably steep, but with pretty consistent terrain and no moguls. Between 3,000 and 4,000 vertical feet to the bottom.

We skied away from the gondola to the top of the first run. David said, "Do you remember that Ajax looks right down into town?"

"Yes," I said. "I only skied here a couple of times because I wasn't good enough, but the view was awesome."

"Point your ski pole toward where you think the closest part of town is," David said.

I pointed out at about forty degrees or so.

"Not quite," he said as he pushed my pole down about a foot. "Right there."

"You're kidding me," I said. Clearly, it was steeper than I thought. "And we're going to ski down this?"

"You'll do fine. Just listen for me. Now push ahead, and your first turn is a right—Now!

"Left, hold, hold, right, hold, left," I heard him say.

We skied down with several breaks for me to catch my breath. I only had a couple of minor falls.

When we got to the bottom I said, "It didn't seem that steep when we were skiing."

"It's wide open and consistent," David said. "I thought you skied it well. Let's do it again while the sun is still on this side of the mountain. It should soften up a bit."

We skied that loop many times, on many ski trips. One day David said, "It's wide open, and there are no other skiers on this run. How would you like to do some free skiing?"

"I'm game."

"I'll call a left turn, then say center line as you pass the fall line, then right turn. That should give you a sense of the rhythm. After I say right, I'll also say on your own. That tells you to make your own turns. You'll only hear me talk if I need to get you back in the center or you need to stop."

"Sounds good."

"OK. Now, push off and left, now center-line, now right, and on your own."

I tried to feel the snow for a bit of a rise that I could turn on, then went left, felt for a rise, then right, and down the run I went. I quickly lost the rhythm David had tried to establish, but I enjoyed the faster rhythm. Right, left, right, left, and on and on.

It was hard work. I was going straighter down the hill than David and I had, and I tried to slow my speed with explosive turns. Not perfect form, but it worked, and it was invigorating.

After that, David and I used this free skiing technique a lot.

"Whenever I see an opportunity for you to free ski," he said, "I'll call center line. That's your cue to listen for me to call a turn and say 'on your own' and start taking your own turns.

I loved the increased freedom and was confident I was alone on the mountain until I heard David say, "hold your next left."

On one of these runs David said, "on your own." I took off for quite a while until I heard him say, "Hold your next right. Do you want to take a break?"

I threw up both of my arms to signal that I needed a break, and David said, "right turn to a stop."

"That was awesome!" I said. "Really fun."

"You stayed right in the fall line until the very end. I counted 120 turns before I lost count. Good skiing."

These runs became our normal morning routine. Sometimes David would announce "We've had 15,000 vertical before lunch. Want to do 25,000 today?"

"My legs are already dead," I answered, but we kept skiing.

One of these runs was the one where Robert Kennedy's son, Michael, was killed several years later. But he was playing football with other family members when he skied into a tree. No risk of me trying that dangerous game.

As the sun moved around to the western side, we'd move with it. Some of those runs made up the bottom part of a World Cup downhill course, and they were almost too difficult to be much fun.

Then came the day that David asked, "Want to ski a double black diamond?"

By then, I'd skied some single black diamonds, and I didn't mind as long as they didn't have moguls.

"I'll give it a shot, if you think I can ski it. What's it called?" I asked.

"Corkscrew. The hardest part is getting to it. We have to go down a very narrow road that I'll have to guide you on. It's not wide enough for me to grab your pole. Once we get through that, the run will be good. It's very steep, but no moguls. It drops right into the west end of town."

He was right about the road being the problem. It had a steep, long, sharp right turn that we had to negotiate. David tried guiding me, but the road was too narrow for me to go back and forth. I soon skied off the road on the uphill, safer side.

"Let's try going side by side, but very slowly," David suggested.

That was a bad idea. The only way to keep our speed down was to stay in a mild snow plow. The tail of my left ski wandered on top of the tail of David's right ski, and I don't know what happened. I took an immediate left turn behind him and skied off the downhill side into a fifteen-foot drop into soft powder. Powder up to my waist! And at a very steep angle.

I'd been totally out of control and didn't think I'd have a safe landing. This escapade frightened me. I struggled to stand up and was panting.

"Are you OK?" David asked.

"I think so. Let me catch my breath."

"What happened?" he asked.

"I got on the back of your ski and spun toward the left edge and went over."

"Yeah, it's pretty narrow. I told you this was the hard part. Can you get your skis off and hand them up to me?"

I took off my skis and was able to hand them up to David. It was hard work, but I eventually found enough footing to climb up to the road.

"The good news is that we're done with this road," David said. "We only need to ski about thirty yards to get to the actual run.

When we got there, I took a few minutes to catch my breath. As I did, I felt over the edge with my pole. It almost felt vertical. *A double black diamond*, I reminded myself.

———■———

I'd already skied an interesting land formation at Alpine Meadows in Lake Tahoe. Within the first several years skiing as a blind person, I was invited to a business meeting at Squaw Valley in Lake Tahoe. I accepted. The meeting was on a Thursday, so I immediately started to investigate the ski resorts in the area to see if any had experience with blind skiers. Close to Squaw Valley—which did not have a blind ski program—was Alpine Meadows. They assured me that they had experience with blind skiers and could accommodate me.

This was my first experience away from Aspen. When I showed up Friday morning, I learned that they assigned separate guides for the morning and the afternoon, rather than for a full day like in Aspen. *OK*, I thought, *we'll see how it goes.*

"Hi Bill. I'm Neil, your guide for this morning. How do you feel today?"

"Nice to meet you. I'm ready to ski Alpine Meadows."

"Let's sit down for a minute and discuss what runs you like to ski and how you like to be guided," Neil said. In Aspen, we went through this same familiarization discussion with any new guide, so this was a good sign.

"I've skied in Aspen," I said, "and I like blue and some black runs, but I generally don't enjoy lots of moguls." We also discussed techniques and preferences getting on and off the lifts. "You'll need to guide me from behind, since I'm a total, and call all the turns," I said.

"What kinds of commands do you want me to use?"

"Tell me what you would normally say. I think the commands need to be what you're used to, so if you need to react quickly to a situation, it will come to you without having to think."

"That sounds like a good idea. I normally call *Left*, and *right*, and *left and right*. And if you need to hold a turn I either say *hold, hold, hold*, or *traverse, traverse*." Is that what you're used to?"

"That's perfect," I said. "You'll probably notice me preparing for the next turn before you say "and," but don't worry. Just keep calling the turns where you think they're appropriate, and I promise to wait for your call before turning," I said.

"OK, let's go ski."

Neil was a good, safe guide, but I quickly got the sense that as I got more comfortable with him, he became a little uncomfortable because I started picking up more speed. I noticed he stopped me fairly often, but we had a good morning.

After lunch, we returned to the office to meet my guide for the afternoon.

"Hi Bill. I'm Billie," a voice said. Who knew that Billie would be a woman?

"Hi Billie. How are you?"

"I'm great. Did you have a good morning with Neil?" she asked.

"It was great."

"Let's discuss your skiing preferences and how you like to be guided," she said.

We then went through the whole discussion about how long I'd been blind. Could I see anything at all? How much had I skied? What kinds of runs did I like? How did I like to be guided?

"I know you're warmed up from this morning," Billie said, "but I want to start on a green run, so we can get familiar with each other.

"Good idea," I said.

We skied the green run and went on to blues. Billie did good, and we skied well, but I had a sense that while she was game, she—like Neil—was also a little uncomfortable. I decided not to mention it at the time, but I stayed conscious of cutting back on my speed and making sure I responded immediately to every command.

At the end of the day, we sat down to get a cup of coffee.

"Billie, you did a great job today, and we skied well together, but can I ask you a question?" I said.

"Sure."

"I sensed you were a little uncomfortable at times. Have you had much experience with blind skiers at Alpine Meadows?"

She paused for a minute. "Thanks for the compliment, but you nailed it. We've had several groups of students from schools for the blind here every year, and I've worked with all of them. But none of them actually knew how to ski. This was my first time to ski with an adult blind skier like we did today."

"Thanks for being honest," I said. "You really did well. Some people don't have the knack for doing this, and they never get it. Others have the knack for it, and are good from the start. You're one of them."

"Thanks for saying that. I was a little nervous when we started, but you make good, quick turns, and I was more comfortable as the day went on," she said.

"I could sense that."

We talked some more, and I learned that she and her husband had moved to Lake Tahoe fifteen years earlier. He'd been injured in a construction accident and was paralyzed from the waist down. He started skiing on a mono-ski and loved it so much that they moved to Lake Tahoe where they both started working with the disabled ski program at Alpine Meadows.

"I would love to move to a ski town and ski every day," I said. "I've been getting in twenty-one or twenty-two days a year for the last couple of years, and I want to keep it up."

"Bill, you asked me a question, and now I have one for you," Billie said. "I'd like to ski with you for the rest of your time out here. Would you consider that?"

I figured that they weren't holding back any other experienced guides, and she'd done well and showed a lot of promise.

"Yes," I said. "That would be great. Changing guides at lunch every day doesn't make sense to me, and we'll do great together."

We skied together the next morning, and Billie became more and more comfortable.

Shortly after lunch, she asked, "Are you ready for something different this afternoon?"

"Sure."

"We're going to the top of the mountain to ski a really fun run. It's steeper than anything we've done yet, but I think you'll do fine." On the lift, she described the run where we were going.

"It's very steep at the beginning, but after a few turns, it gradually gets a little less steep. It's a big, wide-open runout for a mile or so. No obstacles, no bumps. Just make open turns and keep your speed up. Don't over-turn, and we'll have a blast."

We got off the lift, and skied a ridge top to get to the run.

She grabbed my pole and said, "Listen to me. Now come to a slow stop, right . . . here. You're at the top of the run, perpendicular to the hill. Reach down with your left pole and feel how steep it is."

I stuck my pole out at a forty-five-degree angle and lowered it until I felt it hit the hill. It felt almost straight down.

"Is this for real?" I asked.

"Like I said, it's very even terrain with no obstacles," Billie said. "Don't over turn, trust that the hill will become less steep, and control your speed. Let me know when you're ready. A few others are thinking about going, but I think they're waiting for us now."

I took a deep breath. "Let's go," I said.

"Your first turn is a right. Make about four or five wide open turns, and listen for me to call other turns," she said.

Oh my gosh. What a new feeling! Little sense of weight on my skis, making open turns. The snow was pretty hard packed, not fluffy, but I could get a little edge in it. Terrifying! Was there really nothing in front of me?

"Easy right," Billie said. She was right behind me. She continued to call turns, but with lots of delay between the turns. I kept my skis pointed down the hill to keep up my speed as much as I could. I may have skied this fast for a short stretch in the past, but never for this distance. It was exhilarating.

"Easy left . . . easy right," Billie continued. "Now start slowing down, right, and left, and right turn to a stop."

"WhoooooHooooo!" I hollered at the top of my lungs. "That was a blast. I've never skied a run that was anything like that. Was it really as wide open as you said?"

"It was. We never came close to a side of the trail or even another skier. I thought you might like that. I could tell your turns got a little more open as we kept skiing. You looked good. Want to do it again?"

"Sure."

We did it again that day, and several other times over the next two days. Billie became a great guide very quickly, and skiing that wide open, steep run made me a better skier. I had to really trust my guide and keep my skis pointed down the mountain, trusting that I had the control I needed and that the path was clear. It was a different feeling. Now that I had felt it, I could carry it back into my technique on other sorts of terrain.

———■———

Having had this experience, I thought I might be able to ski Corkscrew—that double black diamond run—with my guide, David. But after falling over the edge on the access road, my confidence was shaken. My pole didn't lie; the mountain felt almost vertical.

"Feels steep," I said to David. "Does it flatten out a little as you ski down?"

"Very little," he said. "Just enough that you can get a hold. The snow today is pretty soft, so it's perfect. Ready?"

"OK."

"When you take off," David said, "turn right as you go over the edge. Then you'll be on your own."

It was awesome. It took no more than about ten turns to get to the bottom. Probably a foot of fresh powder. Soft and beautiful.

We skied straight to a lift that was getting ready to close and caught a ride to the top of the gondola to end the day. Corkscrew hadn't been the Look Ma run at Vail that had terrified me twenty years earlier, but it was close—and I'd conquered it!

———————■———————

On other ski trips, I had some "interesting experiences"—a better term, I think, than "close calls." Ginny and I went to Whistler Blackcomb in Canada for a week over the 1999 Christmas break to celebrate the new millennium. The adaptive program in Whistler scheduled guides for me in half-day increments. The first day, the morning guide wasn't so good, but the afternoon guide was really good—a dentist from eastern Canada. He had a take-charge attitude, and we skied well together. He volunteered to ski with me all day for the next several days.

Guide programs often suggest that new volunteers shadow an experienced guide and blind skier for a day to see how it's done. They can also be deployed to block faster skiers from overtaking us when there's poor visibility or converging trails. A young woman shadowed us for a day, then joined us again the next day. As is the normal progression, my guide asked her if she wanted to "drive" me for a bit to see how it felt.

"Sure," she said, and we took off. She did well down a couple of runs, stopping me at the top of each section and gaining confidence. I could hear it in her voice. We continued.

"Left.

"Right

"Left turn to a stop."

Left turn to a stop tells me to come to a comfortable stop, by turning my skis a little to the left and into the hill until I stop. But this time, the hill seemed to slowly fall away from me, so I kept turning more to the left to find the hill and stop. No panic—I was only going a few miles an hour.

"I guess that was a bad place to have you stop," she said. "You went over a little knoll, but no worries. You're actually facing back toward the run, so just push forward, and find the fall line."

As I leaned into my poles to push off, I started sliding backward, not forward.

"What the heck?" I said as I started moving backward more quickly.

SPLASH!

I was now standing in four feet of water and heard, "Don't move, Bill! I'm coming in to get you."

Almost immediately, a small crowd gathered. Several other skiers had seen what happened, and skiers are generally very willing to come to one another's aid. While there's a ski patrol, they are not ever present, and other skiers are often the first responders.

"Is he alright?"

"What happened? I just saw him slide backwards." The voices all piled on top of each other.

"Stay where you are," I said. "I'm OK. What happened?"

"You're in a creek. You apparently stopped on a cornice of snow that overhung the creek. Your weight caused the cornice to collapse. I'm coming in to get your skis off," my dentist guide said.

"Hang on," I said. "Let me see if I can get them off before you get wet too. It's kind of chilly in here." I lifted my right boot and ski and stepped down behind my left boot with my right ski until it released. Huh, still works under water, I thought.

"Got one off," I said. Then I stepped with my left boot behind my right boot and lifted my right heel.

"Got the second one."

Both skis were now lying on the bottom of the creek. I had no idea how to pick them up without getting even wetter, so I ducked under the water and picked them up. Now I was wet from head to toe.

"Come over here and hand me your skis and poles. Keep coming, five more feet."

I sloshed forward several feet and held out my skis.

"Hold the skis up higher," my guide said, talking to me from several feet above the water line.

"Got 'em," he said. "Now we need to get you out of there."

I felt the snowy creek bank in front of me. It went straight up about three feet like a mini-cliff.

"Can you get a toe hold to climb up?"

"Not really," I said as I felt around under water with my ski boots. "There's nothing for me to grab onto to climb out."

"Reach up here, and I'll try to help pull you out," a man—I didn't know who—said. But his footing wasn't good, and I was too heavy to pull out dry, much less soaking wet.

"Is there another guy with you?" I asked. "Can one of you grab each arm and try to drag me out?"

"Yeah," he answered. "Here, reach both your arms up high."

It worked. I was soon standing back on the ski slope, soaking wet, and starting to feel cold as the initial surge of adrenalin wore off. The shivering started.

"How can we get him down?" one of the men asked.

"Someone call the ski patrol! We need a sled to keep him warm and get him down." another said.

"I have a space blanket in my backpack, if that helps. You can have it," someone else said.

"It's going to take a half hour or more to get a ski patrol up here."

Now I was really getting cold and my body was wracked with shivering.

Someone suggested, "We're not too far from the top of the gondola. Maybe he could ride down and get out of the wind."

Silence.

Finally, someone spoke. "It's only about a hundred yards, but how can we get him there without a toboggan?"

"I should be able to ski that far," I said. "I just need to get out of this wind."

"OK," the dentist said. "Let's go quick."

I could feel water sloshing around in my boots. Strange feeling, but we soon got to the gondola and out of the wind.

When we got in the gondola, I asked if anyone had a dry cell phone I could use. "Hi, Ginny," I said when she answered. "Could you get some dry clothes for me and meet me at the office as soon as you can? I got a little wet."

"Wet? What happened? Are you alright?"

"I'll tell you all about it when you get here. I'm fine and am riding down on the gondola."

"Ok. I'll hurry," she said.

When we finally met up, Ginny was not happy, and her nursing instincts kicked in.

"Bill! Your lips are all blue," she said when she saw me. As I stripped out of the wet fleece and outerwear and put on the warm, dry clothes she'd brought me, I told her the whole story.

———⬛———

Another time, I was skiing with Sid, an experienced guide with whom I'd skied many days. We were at Aspen Highlands, the snow was great, and we skied everything from the Merry-Go-Round restaurant down.

The wind was calm that day, and Sid asked, "Do you want to take the next lift up? We can ski down past the restaurant and ride back up at mid-mountain."

"Sure. What's the name of the run up there?"

"Kondahar," Sid said. "It's a blue-black. Pretty steep, but very few moguls. You'll do great."

I'm always a little bit tentative the first time on a run because I don't know what's ahead. Are there double fall lines to contend with? Narrow points that require slowing down? Flat run-outs? These can all mess up the rhythm my guide and I develop.

As we stopped at the top of the run, Sid said, "This whole run is very consistent. Pretty steep, but no big surprises. Let's ski."

That day, the snow on Kondahar was perfect. Soft packed snow that provided great grip, and it was very forgiving.

"Left.

"Right.

"Left.

"Right."

I started leaving my turns a little more down the fall line and picked up more speed. We were soon flying past the restaurant to the gentler green run that took us to the mid-mountain ski lift. We kept up our speed by making the turns more and more open.

"That was a blast!" I said when we got to the lift. "We really bombed down that run."

"Yeah, some slower skiers were looking at us like we were crazy," Sid said. "Want to do it again?" "For sure."

After that, we did laps of those two runs. As we became more and more comfortable with the pitch and the turn radius, we gained more and more speed.

On about the fourth or fifth lap, we blasted past the restaurant and onto the green run at top speed.

"Left.

"Right.

"Left.

"Right"

I was making big, open giant slalom-like turns and enjoying the wind in my face.

"Left!" Sid screamed.

"LEFT! MORE LEFT! MORE LEFT!" Sid hollered at the top of his lungs.

I was traveling right to left on the hill, and turned as sharply as I could without making a hockey stop. I suddenly hit something that felt padded with my right shoulder and was launched into the air. My skis ripped off, and I landed on my butt.

"Are you alright?" I asked as I clambered back up the hill. I assumed I'd clipped another skier. "Are you OK?"

"I'm OK. How are you?" Sid asked.

"I'm fine, but what about the person I hit?"

"That wasn't a person," Sid said, his voice very weak and shaky.

"Then what happened?"

"Do you remember from when you could see that there are padded utility poles down the middle of this run?"

"Oooh. I do."

"After we passed the restaurant, I was watching a beginner skier who was ahead of us on the right side of the run," Sid said. "She was very consistent with her turns, so I wasn't too concerned because we could just pass on her left. Just when I called the last right turn, she headed toward the middle of the run instead of making another right turn. You were headed right at her at about twenty miles an hour faster than she was going. I screamed, 'Left,' and you turned. You missed her but were headed straight for a utility pole."

"That's what I brushed against?"

"Yeah. Somehow you cleared it, but you ejected from your skis and did a flip before you landed fifteen feet down the hill," Sid said. "Are you sure you're alright?" he asked again.

"I'm OK. Just glad I didn't hit someone."

"I can't believe you aren't badly hurt. I thought you were going to ski straight into that pole. Let's get your skis on and get down, but let's take it kind of easy. Alright?"

"Sure."

I could tell Sid was rattled. When we got to the mid-mountain lift, I asked "How about we just go down and get a beer. It's three o'clock, and we can just call it a day."

"That sounds great."

After a couple of beers, Sid admitted he thought he'd really screwed up and had gotten someone hurt.

"I'm happy it's just a good story," I said.

———■———

These stories are memorable, but my close calls were few and far between. The real appeal of skiing is the regular, un-eventful day. Six or more hours of enjoying the day's snow conditions. Skiing all kinds of runs, looking for the ones that have the best snow, fewest number of skiers, and are just the right level of challenge for me. Then we do a few laps of the good ones. Along with skiing, I've gotten to meet what has to be the finest group of people ever, the guides who've invested their time to become great guides. David from Aspen always said, "Hey, if I can loan you my eyes for the day, and we both have a good time, why wouldn't I do that?"

I get a lot of kudos, but the guides really have the tougher job. I can't imagine the stress of meeting someone who claims that they're a blind skier of whatever skill, then going out on the mountain to see how it goes. The guide has to watch where the other person is skiing, try to call turns at the right spots, trust that the blind skier will hear and respond promptly, watch for and avoid other skiers, and always be prepared to direct the blind skier to "crush" or otherwise avoid hazards. While some are ski instructors, the great majority are volunteers who may get a parking pass and a lift ticket for their efforts. Very selfless people.

Their job is tougher than mine. I just have to follow directions and trust the guides. They have to juggle their control of me with the random, busy environment of a ski slope. And all the pieces are moving at the same time.

CHAPTER
TWENTY-ONE

I'd been shot ten months earlier, and now it was time to move from the supportive, understanding world of the medical and blindness community to the real world. It felt surreal to commute to my office in a cab with Darby. Work seemed the same as before, but totally different. Now I had a laptop instead of my old blue-lined legal pads. I had a hand-held cell phone instead of a unit built into my van. I moved into the larger office closer to Kristine. And I had no clients.

At our firm, a senior manager is one level below partner. It can be the most demanding and pressure-packed position, trying to generate enough business to be admitted to the partnership. I had a reasonably successful record of satisfied clients. In a perfect world, those clients would be a source of new engagements, referrals, and references for other opportunities I could develop. But I wondered if this process had been interrupted because of what had happened to me. How would potential new clients react to entrusting their budget and their important, visible projects to a team led by a blind person? There was much to fear, but the time had come to push forward. I would take one step at a time and trust that if I did what I needed to do, I'd be on the right path.

First I had to teach Darby the route from a taxi cab to the building entrance, then the route through that big, open lobby to the elevator button. It only took a few days, and he did great. Better than sneaking behind the planters and against the wall with my cane.

I spent the first couple of weeks getting reacquainted with friends and colleagues in the building. Darby was definitely a conversation piece. Everybody loved him, but I had to teach them not to pet him when he was in harness. Especially people on the elevator in close quarters. I knew he'd look up with those big Labrador eyes and invite a pat on his head.

"That's when he's working, and petting will distract him," I reminded other riders.

There isn't much to do in a consulting firm if you aren't working on a client project. Again, I contacted past clients and colleagues to let them know I was back to work for good and looking for opportunities. But the sales cycle is long, and I was starting from scratch.

One morning the phone rang.

"Bill, its Gary. How are you?"

"I'm doing well, Gary. How are you?" I said.

"I'm good, and everything is going well at Meridia. I got your call a month ago, but didn't call back until we finalized our plans. Do you remember when you did that network design analysis for our computer network? "

"Of course. I hope it's all working well."

"Oh yeah, it's fine. You suggested then that we could probably save some money and gain a lot of functionality if we replaced the telephone systems at all five hospitals. Well, we're ready to do it, and we want you to lead the project."

I was thrilled. The project was right in my sweet spot, and Gary and his boss had been a pleasure to work with.

"That's great, Gary." I said, wondering if he knew what had happened to me. Should I say anything? "There've been a few changes in my life in the last nine months," I said, prefacing a longer explanation.

"I heard about Atlanta. We were all praying for your recovery. You must be doing well since you answered the phone," Gary said.

"It's been an interesting journey. Do you know that I'm blind?"

"Yes. We've followed your progress through some of your KPMG brethren. When can you come to Cleveland and get started?"

We discussed the broad parameters of the first phase, a strategic plan. "I think I have enough information in my files to put together a proposal," I said. "I'll staff it with myself and Linda, a colleague in our Saint Louis office."

We set up a meeting for early the next week.

This was exactly the opportunity I needed to get up and running. It was the blue bird of all blue birds. I couldn't have predicted how any of this journey would unfold, but every step of the way, the right people and opportunities appeared at just the right times.

I only needed to recognize opportunities when they arose and do my part to take advantage of them.

I simply put one foot in front of the other every day.

For the flight to Cleveland, I asked Linda to meet Darby and me at the ticket counter. I was certain that if the cab driver dropped me off at the entrance I had in mind, Darby and I could walk a straight line for sixty feet to the ticket counter. It was straight ahead through the first entrance door.

"Hello, Bill," Linda said as we approached the counter.

"Wow. Darby found it," I said.

We both qualified for business class upgrades, and there were seats available. It was my second flight with Darby, and I was glad he'd have plenty of room. I soon found out that airline employees liked Darby to be comfortable and out of the way, so I often earned an upgrade on flights for which I didn't qualify on my own.

Linda and I went through security together. I put Darby at heel by my left hand, and I held Linda's right elbow—which didn't leave a hand for my briefcase.

"They didn't issue me enough hands to be blind," I often remarked. A soft-sided briefcase with a shoulder strap solved that problem.

We went straight to the meeting with Gary and his colleague at their offices. I introduced Linda, and we spent some time catching up.

"You don't know how much I appreciate this opportunity to work with you," I said.

"We're happy you can help us also, " Gary said. "You made us comfortable with the less expensive solution on the last project, and it saved us $200,000. The system is working great. We're hoping for the same result on this project."

"We'll try our best. Linda and I have worked on several similar projects, so I can promise we'll get through it quickly. And we'll aim to come in below your budget. Plus, you now have Darby to help you."

"Does he have a billing rate, too?" Gary joked.

"No billing rate. Not even expenses, but I was thinking of getting him a frequent flyer number," I said.

Later, as Linda and I prepared to spend a week in Cleveland doing staff interviews, I thought about where I should stay. I usually chose a Marriott Hotel, as was our normal practice, but I thought about having to find my way out of my room, to the elevator to the lobby, and then outside so Darby could relieve himself. Morning and evening. I had no idea if there'd be any grass, or if he would have to "park" in the Marriott driveway. It seemed too complicated.

"I think that staying in a Holiday Inn might be easier for Darby and me," I told Linda. "Close to an outside door and some grass, so I can take Darby out to relieve himself. It would be a lot easier than at the Marriott. Would you be willing to stay there this week?"

"Sure," she said. "Whatever works best for you both."

We stayed at the Holiday Inn, and I got a room on the first floor next to an outside door. It made that first trip with Darby as simple as it could have been. I was still learning about packing food and supplies for him, in addition to my own things.

Early in most strategic planning engagements, we conduct a lot of interviews with the client's staff to learn about their concerns and to trial run possible changes we might suggest. Or, as Andy Rooney said, "A consultant is someone who borrows your watch to tell you what time it is." There's a certain amount of truth to that, but we hopefully bring expertise and judgement to bear on the problems too.

I gave my new laptop a workout during these interviews. I put an ear bud in my ear, and took notes as people spoke. By this time, I'd taken Dr. Barrett's advice and bought several pairs of expensive sunglasses. For the first year or two, the little bit of light I could see sometimes gave me a feeling of vertigo. The sunglasses blocked that light and seemed comfortable. Plus, didn't the stereotype of blind people include sunglasses?

The client managers who hire consultants generally understand the benefit and need for our outside voice and experience on their project. But others in the organization may feel threatened by our involvement. Our first task was to gather the heads of the same departments from each of the five hospitals to find out their concerns. One of the participants was defensive and a little hostile. Linda and I kept on with our questions, like good professionals.

Finally, he said, "I thought you hot shot, laptop using, sunglass-wearing cool consultants were supposed to have all the answers. Why are you asking me?"

Darby was sleeping under the table, and apparently, the man hadn't seen him.

"You know more about what's going on at your hospital than we do," I said. "We're just asking questions to understand your environment and address any concerns you may have."

"Well, OK," he said. He was quiet for the rest of the meeting.

When the meeting broke up, he approached me. "I really feel bad about what I said. My mouth often gets the best of me, so I apologize. After I shot off my mouth, I noticed that you had an ear bud plugged into your computer as you took notes. When I heard a noise under the table, I realized there was a Seeing Eye dog with you."

"No problem," I said. "Don't worry about it."

"You look at everyone when they're speaking, and I would have never known you were blind," he said.

"I'll take that as a compliment."

I was learning that graciousness and generosity served me much better than reacting defensively and building a resentment in such situations. Like this guy, most people have no reason to be hostile toward me as a blind person. The more I can keep my cool, the more I'm able to defuse such rare situations.

We successfully completed the project, and it led to a larger follow-on project, which was also successful. This first project allowed me to get back in the saddle and confirm that I could do my old job. Much of the credit goes to Linda. It would have been very different— and more challenging—without her.

Linda and I built on our experience getting the presentation ready for the bank in Atlanta. She seemed to know intuitively which tasks were better suited to each of our complementary capabilities. If we needed to organize or sort a lot of data, we knew it would take me more time than her. We divided our work based on who could do each task better.

———————

At KPMG, we normally worked in small teams on consulting projects. When I had my sight, I did most of the work myself and asked the other team members to help with certain tasks. I was wrong to think I could do everything better myself. Besides, managing others was an art of its own and required some planning and thought. But now I had to rely on others, which usually meant letting them do their job. And it worked out well, especially for my co-workers. Linda took on more responsibility and served new roles with our clients. My old ways would have held her back. I was learning that being blind was making me a better manager by requiring me to share responsibilities and trust the other professionals around me.

For writing reports, we used our administrative assistant. Kristine had left for a better opportunity, and we tried several others before one of the unassigned administrative support people joined us. Molly was very good, and she quickly became a valuable addition to our small team. She was expert at turning rough drafts into beautiful Power Point presentations that we could add to and polish. It was a pretty efficient system.

With the Meridia Health Systems project behind us, we sold several other projects and were both pulled into larger projects from other practice areas. It's possible that I lost a proposal because I was blind, but I couldn't tell you which one. We won some and lost some. Same as before.

As I'd promised Magid, my old roommate at Lions World, I received comments from clients about how well I functioned and how little blindness seemed to hinder me. They made me blush with pride. It confirmed that my early dreams were materializing.

Linda and I had also worked on a project at Allstate Insurance in Chicago. The firm had a large project to reengineer the data side of the MIS organization. Doug, a Senior Manager from our Radner, Pennsylvania office, was the project leader. He brought Linda and me in to do a similar project with their voice telecom organization.

Getting to know Doug proved to be fortuitous. Over the ensuing months, as Linda's and my careers went in different directions, Doug became my boss. He was my first manager since Tony Lake who had a background and was focused on networking and telecom, data center, and security. The same three areas that Tony identified in 1990, were now called infrastructure throughout the industry. Doug became the lead of KPMG's infrastructure practice for the entire country, except for New York and New England. We worked together until I retired, and he was a great boss and mentor. If I had to rank him and Tony as bosses, I'd say they were tied for first.

After I returned to work, I soon realized that being blind wouldn't prevent me from doing my job. My success, like everyone else's, was based on how well I performed. And I was off to a good start.

In the Spring of 1994, I asked Ginny to marry me. We were married in November. It was a beautiful, simple ceremony at an old church that was often rented out for weddings and receptions. We invited one hundred friends and family and danced late into the night to the music of a local rhythm and blues band. It was a great night. My brother-in-law, Rich, was my best man, and my kids, now nine and ten, and Ginny's daughter were there. And Darby.

I had many great years with Darby by my side, although I seldom took him skiing with me. I didn't think it was fair to leave him in the care of someone at the adaptive ski office or in my hotel room, while I was gone for seven or eight hours. But Darby and I traveled all over the country for my work. He worked for eight years before he told me it was time to retire.

He never put me at risk, but he did become a little sloppy. Sometimes I'd brush a sign post for no reason while walking down a street, or he might meander a little when crossing the street. I'd been warned at The Seeing Eye that this would happen, and it was Darby's way of telling me his working days were over. He remained a wonderful family pet for another four years until an internal tumor took him. Our veterinarian spelled out the options, and I decided to end his suffering.

Ginny, my Dad, and I took Darby to the vet that last day. Dad had become close to several of my dogs over the years, but Darby was special. Dad had been with me for almost all of my journey from the sidewalk in Atlanta to regaining my life, and Darby was a big part of building the full life I now enjoyed. When it was time for that farewell injection, Dad left the room and shed those tears that had been so close in Atlanta. Ginny and I sat on the floor and held Darby as he took his last peaceful breaths. He was my first and last guide dog.

EPILOGUE

I woke up this morning to the sound of our dog moving restlessly in his bed. Ginny had gone on vacation several days ago, and I was home alone.

"Good morning, Flash," I said as I knelt down to pet him. "Let me brush my teeth, and then I'll feed you."

Flash is a beautiful ninety-pound brindle boxer mix with a gentle personality. He loves everyone. He's not a guide dog, but he's sure a great pet.

Downstairs, I fed Flash, then made a cup of coffee and sat down to read the morning paper. Ginny was in Machu Pichu on a guided trip to see the antiquities and flora of Peru. We'd been on a couple of trips to Europe for sightseeing, and we both enjoyed them. A good tour guide can make the country and its culture come alive. I'll never forget getting a sense of the Eiffel Tower by feeling one of its legs. But it's also nice for Ginny to travel with a group to other attractions, while I save my vacation budget for more skiing.

I made scrambled eggs and bacon for breakfast and pulled up my calendar to see what I had to get done that day. Ten o'clock workout with my trainer at Sports Medicine Training Center, a local physical therapy and fitness business. I looked forward to my workout and usually had lunch afterward at The Block, a nearby restaurant.

After cleaning up from breakfast, I dressed for my workout and went back downstairs to check my email.

Nothing pressing, but I responded to a couple of friends. I loaded up my fanny pack with my digital book reader, iPhone, and wallet, and said goodbye to Flash. The gym was about a twenty-minute walk, but I left a little early.

I went out the back door and down the back sidewalk with my cane. Up four steps and out the gate to the driveway. I headed toward the street and located the sidewalk. *Tap, tap, tap, tap.* Left turn for fifteen steps, then I turned right and listened for traffic before I crossed.

When the coast was clear, I stepped off the curb, crossed the street, and found the sidewalk on the cross street. After a couple of blocks, a voice said, "Hi Bill. How are you and Ginny doing?"

"Doing well, Marcy, but she abandoned me this week." Marcy was a woman I'd gone to school with from kindergarten through high school, and she happened to live a few blocks away. "She's on a vacation with the Botanical Garden crowd."

"Where are you off to today?"

"Working out again, and I'll probably get lunch at The Block," I said. "See you later."

"I'll probably still be working in the yard when you come back by," Marcy answered.

Four or five blocks later, I came to the main street and waited on the curb for an opportunity to cross. When it was clear, I crossed and went another block to the building with the gym on the third floor. I found the glass front of the building with my cane and a little further, the revolving door. Through the door, down the hall and into the elevator. I pressed the button for the third floor. When the door opened, Kelly, the receptionist, said "Good morning, Bill. How are you?"

"I'm fine. Is Mike here yet?" I asked. Mike was the

trainer I'd worked out with for several years.

"He just got here, so take a seat, and I'll tell him you're here."

"Hey, Bill," I heard a few minutes later. "Ready to get started?" Mike asked.

"You bet."

I put my cane in my right hand and found his elbow with my left. Mike always designed my workouts to fit my lifestyle. In the fall, we focused more on leg and balance exercises—as well as overall fitness—to get me ready for ski season. Today, he'd really loaded up my legs. When we finished, I thanked him and found the door.

I went back out to the street and listened for an opportunity to cross. When it was clear, I crossed and turned left. *Tap, tap, tap, tap* until I came to some chairs and tables out on the sidewalk. I walked around them and went in the front door.

"Hi, Bill," Amy, the manager, said. "By yourself today?"

"Yep, just me. How've you been?" I put my left hand out, and her elbow found it and showed me to a table.

After lunch, my waitress showed me to the front door, and Amy said "Bye, Bill."

I followed the same route home, but Marcy wasn't outside anymore. I was happy to have the afternoon to finish a book I was reading by C. J. Box. I turned on some music in the background and sat down to read.

My friend, Tom, called around 4:00 p.m. and asked if I had plans for dinner. "Not really," I said.

"I'll pick you up around six o'clock. I know Ginny's out of town, and I found a new restaurant you'll enjoy," he said.

"Sounds great. I'll meet you in the driveway at six."

The restaurant was very good, and I was glad for the company at dinner. Afterward, Tom dropped me off at home, and I went inside to read a little more and get ready for bed.

As I got in bed, I reflected on how grateful I was for the life I had today. This is what I'd wanted all along—a normal life. A life where I could be independent and do the things I wanted to do when I wanted to do them. A life where I didn't have to rely on others to take care of me. A life where I would contribute in the same ways—and maybe even better—than I had before the shooting. In fact, I'd worked for almost twenty more years before I retired. I was an independent man and had never lost that identity.

Many people are curious about my blindness. "Were you blind since birth?" they ask. "Can you see anything?"

"It's from a random shooting by someone I didn't know," I answer.

"Oh, that's terrible. I'm so sorry," they respond.

"Don't be!" I say. "I'm the luckiest person you'll run into today. I should have been killed, not just blinded. I had no other injuries, and I very quickly accepted that I was blind. I had great support from my family and friends, a job that I could still do, and an employer who let me come back to give it a try. My world is just as big and broad as it ever was."

In the early years following the shooting, I sometimes wondered *What if?*

What if I'd taken a taxi to the airport rather than walked to the MARTA station? What if I'd scheduled a different flight? What if we'd been five minutes earlier—or later?

One thing is for certain: I wouldn't have been shot or blinded. At least not that day. And being shot changed my life forever.

Some things in life are simply random, out of your control, a roll of the dice, the luck of the draw. Regardless, we all must play the hand we are dealt. The question is will you control your challenges, or will you allow them to control you? You'll either live life, or life will live you.

Had I not been shot, would life have been easier? Probably. Would I have been happier? That's questionable. One thing is certain: being shot and everything that happened as a result—all the trials and tribulations—have made me a far stronger and better person.

I hope this book provides some strength in your time of need when the odds seem stacked against you, some hope in the future regardless of the situation you find yourself in, some courage to face your challenges and, most of all, the understanding that there is much to be grateful for.

There's *always* a little light.

ACKNOWLEDGMENTS

On every step of my journey, I've been presented with the most wonderful and helpful people. Exactly the right person came into my life at precisely the right time. The encouragement, friendship, and knowledge offered by each of them kept me going. Rather than list all their names here, I've mentioned most of them in this book, and I hope they all know how important they were—and are—to me.

Most important is my wife Ginny, who's been with me almost every step of the way. She's made my life easier by being her loving and helpful self every day.

I'm grateful for Ginny and all the others. Without you all, I wouldn't have the life that I have today.

ABOUT THE AUTHOR

BILL JOHNSON lives in Saint Louis, Missouri, with his wife, Ginny. He successfully completed his career with KPMG and BearingPoint as a management consultant and is now retired. His children, Chris and Kelly, are now adults. Ginny has an adult daughter, also named Kelly, and through her, they have four grandchildren.

In addition to his love of snow skiing, Bill enjoys reading, listening to music, working out, spending time with friends and family, and serving the disabled community. And, of course, he will always be a dog lover.

CPSIA information can be obtained
at www.ICGtesting.com
Printed in the USA
FSHW021715140321
79437FS

9 781735 802138